DEVLIN'S
BOATBUILDING

Devlin's Boatbuilding

How to Build Any Boat
the Stitch-and-Glue Way

Samual Devlin

International Marine
Camden, Maine

Published by International Marine®

20 19 18 17 16 15

International Marine/
Ragged Mountain Press

A Division of The **McGraw·Hill** *Companies*

Printed in the United States of America.

Library of Congress Cataloging-in-Publication Data

Devlin, Samual.
    [Boatbuilding]
    Devlin's boatbuilding : how to build any boat the stitch and glue
way / Samual Devlin
        p.   cm.
    Includes index
    ISBN 0-07-157990-7 (alk. paper)
    1. Boatbuilding. 2. Wooden boats—Design and construction.
I. Title.
VM351.D48   1995   *95-39678*
623.8'2023—dc20   *CIP*

Questions regarding the content of this book
should be addressed to:

International Marine
P.O. Box 220
Camden, ME 04843

Questions regarding the ordering of this book
should be addressed to:

The McGraw-Hill Companies
Customer Service Department
P.O. Box 547
Blacklick, OH 43004
Retail customers: 1-800-262-4729
Bookstores: 1-800-722-4726

Devlin's Boatbuilding is printed on acid-free paper.

Printed by Quebecor Printing, Fairfield, PA
Design and Production by Dan Kirchoff
Edited by Jonathan Eaton, Ted Hugger, Tom McCarthy

DEDICATION

There is no road map a dreamer can follow to become a boat designer and wooden boat builder. You just have to keep your pilot light of inspiration shielded, and recognize when the flames of creativity need to be expressed. The world sends many ill winds to blow out the light. Money is probably the chief one; figuring out how to make money building wooden boats remains one of the most difficult challenges of all. The necessary evils of taxes, licenses, bureaucracies, and, today, all the required ecological permits constitute another. And finally, strange as it seems, to make a living designing and building wooden boats you need to sell your creations—market them and indeed stand by them for an inordinate amount of time. Many customers have only a sketchy understanding of what efforts it takes to design and build boats for a living.

With these pitfalls besetting my career, I have found that I am only as good as the people around me. So I must give thanks to my parents for allowing me enough adversity in life to toughen my hide, and enough nurturing to inspire me to keep going.

To my wife, Liz, who has shared my dreams for all these years, struggling side by side with me so that we could live our lives the way we wanted. Our lives today are the results of our own labors, and it's been a strange and wonderful path.

To the workers who have stood by my side, lived with my many moods, and kept perspective on the dream. Especially Jim Henson, Randy Foster, and Joel Mill.

To my many customers, who with their hard-earned money allowed me to follow my dream, and who had the patience to wait for their boats.

And in no small part, to a world of interesting and inspiring boats. To me, boats are like fine wine or music: They live in the hearts of designers, builders, and owners. They can elevate our spirits to a higher plane. If I can accomplish one thing in life it would be to have elevated someone else's spirits with my own creations.

Thank you all for the privilege of a few moments.

CONTENTS

INTRODUCTION:
THE MAGIC OF BOATS

Have you ever considered building a boat? Have you wondered whether the dream of making a boat for yourself was attainable? For me, there is always a magic to boat-building. It starts with little more than the right dream and the right motivation. When I begin to consider building a new boat, I usually imagine some beautiful place on the water. I sense the fresh wind in my face, the warmth of the sunshine, and try to imagine how the boat handles and moves. Surely there is no other advantage to the exercise than the power of the dream to get going. But that advantage is a huge one; the tools and materials are important, but it's the dream that sees you through to the end of the project.

Few things are more satisfying than crafting a pile of rough wood into a beautiful, graceful boat. It is a soul-satisfying psychological and physical adventure. For me it is the essence of creative expression, and anyone can benefit from it. It is so often hard to derive lasting satisfaction from our jobs. The hours would seem shorter and the stress more manageable if we could more often *see* what we're accomplishing. Well, a boat is a living structure that reflects the builder and his or her spirit. As it takes shape you can stand back and survey it with pride, and see what you've created with your own hands.

Building your own boat will be an emotional roller-coaster ride; your energy level and enthusiasm will soar to astounding heights, and just as quickly, plummet to frightening depths. Keeping this phenomenon in perspective is critical from the start, because you'll have days when you gravely doubt the worth of the whole project. Take advantage of the low points in your enthusiasm by turning your attention to something else for a few days. You can then return refreshed and motivated. But don't go away for too long; you may lose interest in the project altogether. Learn to pace yourself.

Finally, strive to keep things under control. I have always kept in mind that the boat I was building would have to be sold someday. You should do this, too—even if selling your pride-and-joy is the furthest thing from your mind. It's all too easy to spend too much money and time on a given stage in the building process. If you keep in perspective the boat's salability, you're more likely to set realistic limits on the actual costs and labor involved. If you think of this boat as the first and only boat you will ever make, you're likely to mismanage the whole project. You'll have cost overruns, and you will find yourself bogged down by an obsessive desire to have everything perfect. Set specific time and budget constraints, and hold to them as you move through the building process.

You may be wondering whether building a boat is within your capabilities. I haven't a doubt: With the right dream, the right design, and the right motivation, anyone can build a wonderful boat. What follows is my attempt to explain the stitch-and-glue method of boatbuilding. It is readily approachable. Bring only your dreams and your enthusiasm. The boat you build will strengthen and reflect your inner spirit, and like me you might find that designing and building wooden boats is a fine thing to do with one's life.

THE ADVANTAGES OF
STITCH-AND-GLUE BOATBUILDING

The differences between conventional plywood-on-frame and stitch-and-glue construction are significant. To better understand the differences between the two, contrast the structural dissimilarities of an early biplane and a modern jet airliner. The biplane was made up of frames and spars over which was stretched a thin skin. The jet airliner's structure, on the other hand, is much simpler, with a stressed aluminum skin rigidly attached to bulkheads and spars to create a single unit. A boat built by attaching plywood planking to lumber frames is most similar to the biplane; a stitch-and-glue boat more closely resembles the jet airliner—a homogeneous structure in which the skin bears the primary stresses.

The basic argument for stitch-and-glue construction is that it uses fewer parts and that epoxy is used to bond and seal the parts to achieve a stronger, monocoque (one-piece) boat. The initial construction is quicker and easier, uses fewer parts, and requires no building molds. And in the long term, the boat is much easier to maintain.

Looking back over my own development in boatbuilding, and considering the advantages and disadvantages of the many forms of construction I've used, I find my memory foggy as to why I chose one form over another. In the beginning, I was simply working out the differences and identifying the problems of each form of construction. I knew that working with natural wood products was appealing, and I knew I wanted to use wood products in an ecologically sound manner. A boat built of wood has a spirit that is easy to see and feel, but much harder to define.

Almost all boatbuilding methods require expensive tooling. Production fiberglass boats have their elaborate plugs and molds. Traditional plank-on-frame or cold-molded wooden boats require complicated building molds. This expensive tooling generally stops much of the evolution of an individual boat design. Stitch-and-glue construction does not bear this initial burden. With no building molds or tooling to consider, a stitch-and-glue design has a chance to constantly evolve and improve—and that's important. I believe that any design can use refinement, and as my work has evolved, I have found ways to increase the ability of the

1

stitch-and-glue boat to suit its purpose and meet its owner's performance requirements.

When I began to get serious about boatbuilding, my first hurdle was finding shop space and lining up the necessary tools. There seemed to be no way to avoid these expenses, and just as surely, no way to be efficient without them. There was a great temptation to toss away all my ideas about innovative boatbuilding and stick to the traditional small wooden boats, which needed fewer power tools. I know that shop space, the cost of tools, and other financial concerns shaped and formed my earliest choices in boatbuilding. With less initial investment, I could have built traditional skiffs and respectable, small wooden, plank-on-frame boats, although I

was intimidated by my lack of skills in the beginning. But in hindsight, these influences were beneficial, as access to building materials and a gradual accumulation of quality tools indirectly steered me to the stitch-and-glue construction format.

When I began building boats, marine plywood was readily available in a variety of thicknesses, and in lengths up to 16 feet. It was during these early years that I began wiring together plywood panels and reinforcing the joints and seams with epoxy. I was totally unaware of others using similar methods, and it was only later that I discovered similar technologies were in use in Australia, New Zealand, and Europe. Little was ever written or published about such efforts, and in retrospect, I'm glad I didn't know about them. I was free to work out

Figure 1-1. A 7-foot 6-inch Polliwog dinghy.

Figure 1-2. A 15-foot 2-inch Nancy's China D.C. out for her first sail.

Figure 1-3. The author rows a 17-foot 2-inch Oarling on Seattle's Lake Union.

my own assumptions and refine my methods in isolation, uninfluenced by others' prejudices. Maybe the greatest consequence of that experience was that it forced me to develop my own style, and I constantly worked toward new and interesting designs.

At first, I simply wanted to work in wood and natural products. I wanted to have good-looking, sturdy boats. I wanted a boatbuilding method that would be relatively inexpensive. The more I worked with plywood, wiring, and epoxies, the more convinced I became that stitch-and-glue boats could be built stronger and easier, and would require less maintenance than other boatbuilding methods.

But I was also aided by the economy and by circumstances that were much bigger in scope and importance than a young

Figure 1-4. A 22-foot Surf Scoter awaits another season of cruising on Puget Sound.

man's wanting to build wooden boats for a living. Although creative, ingenious pioneers had introduced the techniques of mass production to wooden boatbuilding at several points in the 20th century, it was the advent and proliferation of fiberglass boatbuilding that introduced mass-production possibilities to a host of builders. "Boatbuilding" almost turned into boat assembly, and almost became extinct in the process.

But the expense of tooling for a fiberglass boat allows only an occasional and restricted journey from inspiration to final product, and floods the market with similar-looking boats. As time went by, in spite of the mass production of fiberglass boats, a growing segment of the boating public started to search for an alternative, creating a niche market that clamored for innovative design, modern materials technology, and better-built boats. In the early days of my career, the fact that my boats were wooden was an impediment to selling them. But there have been some real shake-ups in the production glass boat market. Today, the experienced consumer realizes that fiberglass boats will not last forever, and that they have their own unique faults and shortcomings. Gradually, wood/epoxy composite boats have picked up a distinct marketing advantage as buyers become better informed and less influenced by slick advertising and flashy showroom models.

Another great thing about stitch-and-

Figure 1-5. A 24-foot 6-inch Black Crown, with inboard diesel engine, slowly motors about on Lake Union.

glue building is that you can get by with a minimum of tools. You need little more than a circular saw, a sander/polisher/grinder, a block plane, a framing square, a level, and a tape measure. With these simple and inexpensive tools you can build a lot of boat. The most basic stitch-and-glue boat simply requires cutting plywood panels, stitching the panels together, and then fiberglassing the seams with epoxy. When the seams have cured, you pull the wires, sheathe the exterior with epoxy and fiberglass cloth, and use the sander-polisher to smooth out the edges. With the addition of seats and gunwale reinforcement, you're ready for paint and finishing work. It's no more complicated than that.

Do not allow yourself to be put off by the misconception that it's hard to build a stitch-and-glue boat. It's no harder and no more complicated than building a garden shed. There are no molds, and there are few preliminary steps, since you begin immediately to set up the hull. With stitch-and-glue construction, there is no need for the shipwright skills of traditional boatbuilding methods. At the same time there is enough depth to the medium that even the most experienced boatbuilder can find satisfaction. Plywood is easy to work with, and a forgiving material. It utilizes all of wood's strengths, while minimizing its weaknesses. Since there is no need for complicated framing, you will be amazed by the simplicity and speed of building a stitch-and-glue boat.

2

SETTING UP SHOP

YOUR WORKSHOP

You need a dry, sheltered workshop to build your boat. Look at the full dimensions—length, width, and height—of the boat you intend to build. Using those dimensions, imagine the rough outline of the boat and its major components on the shop floor. Add a minimum of three feet to all sides to allow enough room to walk comfortably around the assembly procedures. If your garage or workspace is too small for the boat's dimensions, find another space or temporarily enlarge your building to accommodate the project. Remember, depending upon its size, your boat can take a considerable time to build and will tie up your garage or other valuable workspace.

Good work requires ample lighting, and a well-lit shop is a safe shop. To protect

Figure 2-1. The 29-foot Means of Grace design under construction at the Devlin shop.

tools, prevent the wood stock from warping, and promote proper curing of the epoxy, you'll need a dry shop. If you don't have an enclosed work area, there is a greater chance that your work will not cure properly or that excessive moisture will become trapped in the wood and eventually weaken the structure. Eliminate the hassle factors; it takes time to set up before you begin each work session. You'll want to get to work quickly and easily and be able to work in short blocks of time. Some of my best work is done in well-motivated spurts.

Heat is far more important than you might think. Modern epoxies demand curing time, and the shorter that time, the better. The warmer the workshop, the shorter the cure times. Delayed cure times can lead to contamination, dust, or insects fouling the surfaces. Your own comfort is important, too. Warm hands work better than cold hands, and if you are comfortable, your patience and attitude will be more attuned to the work at hand.

Your workspace should have ample room for your tools, and its layout should be conducive to easy cleaning. Cutting, sanding, and many other steps of boatbuilding create a great deal of dust. It is mandatory to clean often—in fact every evening—to avoid kicking up dust during the critical stages of epoxy use and painting. Get into the habit of constantly cleaning and picking up after yourself.

I often live with my tools in less-than-ideal conditions. I like my tools in well-

Figure 2-2. Workbench and storage area shows a bit of the typical boatshop clutter.

organized storage cabinets or stored on easily visible wall racks. A sturdy workbench is an indispensable tool, with two vises to double-clamp long stock. While we are dreaming here, the workspace could have a wood stove for burning up scraps, and a stereo to soothe the soul. The more comfortable and homelike your shop, the greater the chances you'll choose an evening of boatbuilding over an evening in front of the television set. But bear in mind that you must be realistic about your time and energy, and the shop is a means to an end, not an end in itself. I would rather get going on a boat project in a less-than-ideal shop than be hopelessly mired in the quest for a perfect workspace.

TOOLS

The avid boatbuilder will find no limit to the tools available, and no bottom in the wishing well. Temper what you want with what you truly need, and then pare the list to what you can afford.

The most fundamental advice is this: Spend good money on good tools. Avoid buying poorer grades of tools, and wait longer, if you must, to buy good quality. Professional-grade tools balance better, run smoother, last much longer, and are more enjoyable to use. The better the tool, the more likely you are to achieve high levels of craftsmanship. If you are spending hard-earned money on the best boatbuilding materials, why not use the best tools on those materials?

Your initial list of tools can be as simple or complex as you choose. An adequate collection can be quite small, since stitch-and-glue construction requires an absolute minimum of tools.

The first consideration is whether you prefer hand or power tools. Your costs will be less if you choose hand tools, but your work will be much slower. Of course there are several power tools you'll find absolutely indispensable.

Sander

The most used and abused power tool in my shop is a Makita #9207 sander-polisher. I consider a sander-polisher a real must—even for the small builder—to create a uniformly finished boat. This slightly smaller

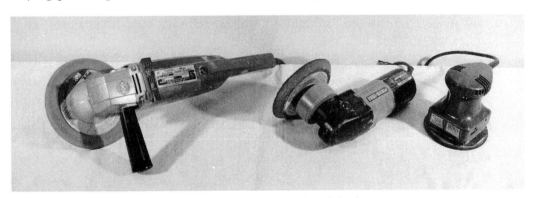

Figure 2-3. The workhorses of the sanding department, from left: the Makita 9207 disc sander, Porter-Cable Random orbital sander, and Makita palm sander.

version of a metal grinder is lighter and runs at slower speeds (1,500 to 3,200 rpm), an important consideration for boatbuilding. It can turn slowly enough to hold the sandpaper and it won't burn wood as quickly as the larger, faster metal grinders. Used with a soft sanding pad and 8-inch, 3M Stickit (or equivalent) disc sandpaper, the Makita will easily handle all your basic sanding needs.

Block Plane

Every boatbuilder should have a good block plane. My father always had a simple-looking block plane in his workshop, and when I began boatbuilding, I was convinced I could do better. So motivated, I headed off to the nearest hardware store with its vast selection of tools. I looked at everything from simple low-angle block planes like my father's to wonderfully specialized and complex tools. I selected the most complicated-looking and expensive model, complete with all the bells and whistles. It had adjustments and little levers for every imaginable need, and I was sure this block plane would cut wood better than anything I had ever held in my hands before. As soon as I returned home, I sharpened the factory edge and placed a beautiful, straight-grained piece of yellow cedar in a bench vise. In my mind's eye, I could already see the long, smooth curls of shavings peeling off the block of wood. But what a rude awakening. The plane iron tore into the wood, digging in with every stroke. I shortened the blade depth and tried again. Now it simply choked the slot between the blade and the body of the plane with wood chips—still no smooth shavings. No matter what I tried, this marvelous plane would not produce acceptable results. It seemed to have been designed by a fiend to gouge and mangle wood. Frustrated and chastened, with my tail between my legs, I went back to the hardware store and picked out a block plane just like my Dad's.

I have never found a block plane better than the Stanley #118, which I bought that day on my second try. It is the perfect low-angle block plane for finishing plywood edges and doing all basic boat construction planing. Stay away from the bells and whistles. The Stanley #118 does the job and is all the builder really needs.

Power Saws

There is a vast array of power saws from which to choose, including handheld jig-

Figure 2-4. One of the simplest and finest hand tools available to the boatbuilder: the Stanley #118 low-angle block plane.

saws, saber saws, circular saws, bandsaws, and various table saws.

A jigsaw can double as a scroll saw and a poor man's bandsaw. I have found the Bosch #1581 to be a fine tool with sufficient blade adjustments to allow quick cutting and multiple angles and bevels.

You'll need a circular saw to cut plywood panels. With a carbide-tipped blade, the circular saw will even cut large-radius curves in plywood. Buy a 7¼-inch model to work with thicker stock, rather than a 6¼-inch.

I cut my teeth on my Dad's old heavy-duty worm-drive Skilsaw. It was an expensive tool, and when the time came to purchase my own, the temptation to cut corners was impossible to resist. My new saw was a direct-drive sidewinder type, with the blade set on the right-hand side of the housing. To use it, because I'm right-handed, I had to lean over the saw to view the cut line. This put my eyes in line with the dust blowing up from the cut and made it nearly impossible to cut a straight line. Sometimes the saw would bind and rip itself out of the cut with frightening force. So, just as I had with the hand plane, I finally went out and spent my hard-earned money on a proper worm-drive saw.

Bandsaw

While it is not an absolute necessity, after you've worked on your project awhile you'll find yourself waking in the middle of the night longing for a bandsaw. And once you've used one, you won't be able to imagine how you ever lived without it.

I have a Powermatic 14-inch bandsaw, and it's a real beaut. These saws don't seem to be as common as some of the Rockwell or Delta models, but for my

Figure 2-5. A worm-drive Skilsaw, left, and the Bosch #1581 jigsaw.

Figure 2-6. A pair of Milwaukee Magnum Holeshooters. (Note the epoxy buildup on the left one, an often-used tool.)

money, there is no better bandsaw on the market. I buy a bandsaw based on the blade guides more than any other feature. Good bearing-type blade guides ensure an easier, more precise cut.

Table Saw

A table saw can be another valuable asset in your shop. I have a Rockwell Unisaw; although a fine tool, it has an appetite for starter capacitors—at about $75 a pop. But this saw cuts strong and straight. Buy a heavy saw with as big a motor as possible. I haven't found horsepower to be an issue with bandsaws, but with table saws, horsepower is cutting power.

Good blades can make or break a table saw, so buy carbide-toothed blades with as many teeth as possible. Also note that there are different types of blades for different cuts—buy a good crosscut blade for plywood work and a good rip blade for resawing dimensional wood.

Drill

A good power drill is a must for stitch-and-glue construction, and I have found that the ½-inch Magnum Holeshooter, made by Milwaukee Tool Company, is the best of the many choices. It is nicely balanced and will handle every job. Along with the drill motor, buy a drill index, with bit sizes from $\frac{1}{16}$ to ½ inch in increments of $\frac{1}{32}$ inch. I prefer high-speed, steel twist bits for general work, but I have also used brad-point bits with good results. The latter are designed especially for wood and for boring flat-bottomed holes. The brad-point bits are rarely available in anything but full sets and are quite expensive, but are worth the investment.

Hammer

Every boatbuilder needs a hammer. I keep a light hammer—preferably a 13-ounce—for delicate work, and a 16- to 20-ounce hammer for heavier pounding. Vaughan manufactures the nicest hammers in these weight ranges. Look for good balance, preferably wooden handles, and fine machining on the heads. And try to avoid pulling out large, deeply driven nails with a wooden-handled hammer; you'll likely as not break it. Use a prybar or a crowbar.

Sharpening Stone

Keep a good sharpening stone handy. The planes, chisels, knives, and other blades used in boatbuilding all need constant attention to function properly. Rather than sending them out for sharpening, learn to care for your blades yourself.

There are many stones available, but I much prefer the diamond-type, which has a metallic-looking, hole-filled face glued to a chunk of plastic. Small diamond grains are embedded in the metal face, and the holes allow the minute sharpening residues to free themselves from the surface. This is the most versatile of sharpening stones; DMT makes the best of these. Water, usually the recommended lubricant, rusts the stones quickly, so I use a light oil such as WD-40 instead. Kerosene also works. I mounted the stone on my workbench with screws to keep it from moving around, and have made a box lid to keep shop dust from fouling its face.

Speaking of sharpening tools, it's nice to have a stropping leather to remove the burr after a workout on the stone. I keep a 24-inch finished-leather strop handy, and know from experience that a couple of swipes on it does wonders for any cutting edge. Actually, any old finished-leather belt will double as a fine strop, and its buckle makes a handy fastener for belaying one end while stropping.

Other Tools

Find a good pair of pliers. Large lineman-type pliers are the best for cutting and twisting the wire you're going to use. Buy the 9-inch size with a wire cutter built into the side of the jaws. It's important to find a pair of pliers that feels comfortable in your hands, since you'll be using them a great deal in the wiring process. This is a top-priority tool.

You'll need a small knife for myriad tasks. For years I used a Swiss Army knife, but after dropping yet another into the briny deep, I decided to search for a better alternative. I finally settled on a good rigging knife. This companion-on-my-hip had to be durable and hold a good edge, yet compact enough to fit my hand perfectly. I had a great knife made by Adrienne Rice of Madrona Knives, Route 1, Box 1230, Lopez Island, Washington, 98261. It's small enough to avoid that Daniel Boone look, and it's great not having to fish around in my pocket for a folding knife.

You'll need a framing square for drawing the station lines during the lofting process. A simple L-square with inch gradations, or a 50-inch drywall T-square is adequate, although any size can be used along with battens to extend the station lines. I find that a straight, stiff, 50-inch wooden batten with a simple framing square is all I really need.

Pick up a retracting tape measure at least 25 feet long. The Stanley Powermatic is just the ticket. Its inch-wide blade will extend 10 feet or so and remain straight while unsupported. You will do a lot of chine-to-chine and sheer-to-sheer measuring to true up the hull. One hint: Take care that you slow the blade when retract-

Figure 2-7. A rigging knife—every boatbuilder should have one.

ing it into the case. I have seen the ends break off as a result of high-speed retraction. I have never found folding rulers to be of much use, so to my mind, they are better left out of your active toolbox.

You'll need a good compass. Buy one that has 10- or 12-inch legs and allows you to insert a pencil. You'll rely on your compass for scribing the bulkheads and for fitting various boat parts. Try a used-tool dealer, since the best compasses are the older models. An alternative might be to buy a set of dividers and tape a pencil to one leg, although you'll need to retape each time you sharpen the pencil.

To keep things straight and level, add a plumb bob, a chalkline, and a 2- or 3-foot level to your toolbox. I use my plumb bob for truing up the bulkheads and maintaining the vertical alignment of the hull during construction of the larger boats. There's also a new electronic tool on the market called the Smartlevel. Although

there is a bit of a learning curve to use one of these, once mastered, it is a true joy.

Get a pair of scissors to cut out cardboard or paper patterns, fiberglass cloth and tape, and peel ply. Look for heavy-duty shears rather than light sewing scissors. Some might find it easier to use a razor blade or utility knife when cutting fiberglass tape.

A well-fitted dust respirator is an important tool that should be part of your basic kit. Your boatbuilding career will be a very short one if you don't take care of your lungs. While I may not be able to afford a dust collector for my shop, I can certainly afford to spend $35 for a good organic vapor canister respirator. We've tried many types in our shop over the years, and the current favorite is a 3M 6000 series—an affordable, lightweight, and comfortable dust mask. It comes either with twist-on cartridges or with lighter weight twist-on prefilters. I clean my face-

Figure 2-8. A full-face-mask respirator for spray painting, left, and a canister filter respirator.

piece in the dishwasher every week and replace prefilters at the same time. The face mask is $12.65, with a pack of two prefilters for $4.35; cartridges are $11.45.

One of the most visible differences between professionally built and amateur-built boats is the detail in the finishwork. That means shaped moldings, chamfered edges, and rounded corners on the boat's wood trim. A router will give you the ability to mill a variety of shaped wood parts. I rely on a heavy-duty, 3-hp Makita #3612BR router mounted on a base bolted to the table of my table saw. For handwork, I use a smaller Porter-Cable, model 1001.

Another nice-to-have tool is a jitterbug or vibrating sander, invaluable for smoothing surfaces prior to painting and varnish-ing. I use a Makita B04510, and, due to the demands of my shop, keep several spares in reserve. Random orbit sanders are another excellent choice. I have several Porter-Cable 333s in the shop, and these have worked very well.

There are many other tools that can greatly ease building but are certainly not required. Those worthy of special mention include a surface planer and an air compressor. If your budget will not stretch, remember that you can always rent them. Start small with a minimum of tools, and if boatbuilding grows on you, so will your tool inventory.

I will spare you the full dissertation, but I have found some of my best tools at garage sales and flea markets. Look for specialty-

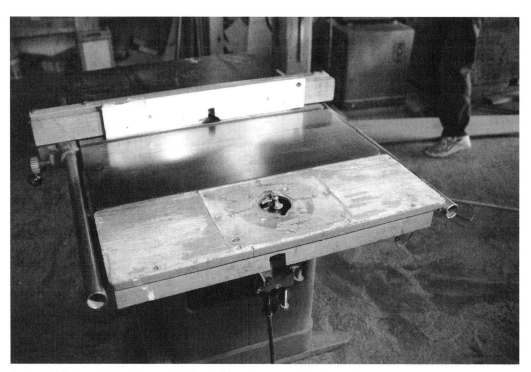

Figure 2-9. A router setup on a tablesaw base is a versatile option to a fixed shaper.

tool buyers in your area. They have experience and provide the best advice about the variety and quality of each tool. I have been thoroughly delighted by finds (in some cases, almost steals) at used-tool dealers. There are also tool reconditioners who specialize in older stationary power tools, which are sturdier—often heavier cast iron—and promise longer service than the newer, lightweight models. Shopping the alternative tool market is good fun and well worth the time; just don't let it interfere with your boatbuilding time.

Basic Tool List (Amateur Builder)

Sander-polisher: Makita #9207 SPC, variable speed (1,500 to 3,200 rpm), 3M 8-inch soft backing pad, 3M Stickit sanding discs of 80- and 150-grit (8-inch diameter)

Block plane: Stanley #118

Jigsaw: Bosch #1581VS Orbital Action

Circular saw: Skil model 77 (13-amp motor) or Black and Decker 7¼-inch worm-drive

Drill: Milwaukee 0234-1 Magnum Holeshooter, ½-inch, 5.4-amp, 0 to 850 rpm

Drill bit index: ¹⁄₁₆- to ½-inch high-speed steel bits

Hammer: Vaughan, 13- and 20-ounce sizes

Pliers: 9-inch Crescent #2050-9C, lineman's type with side cutters

Tape measure: Stanley #33-425 Powerlock, 25-foot

Vibrating sander: Makita BO4510 palm sander or Porter-Cable 333 random-orbit finish sander

Sharpening stones: diamond-type, DMT (325 coarse grit for general work, 600 fine grit, 220 extra-coarse grit)

Square: 24-inch framing square or 48-inch drywall T-square

Compass: 8-inch loose-leg dividers

Bevel gauge: 8-inch metal

Plumb bob: 6- or 8-oz.

Level: Smartlevel electronic level or spirit-bubble type, 24- or 36-inch

Chalkline: Stanley 50-foot

Rigging or pocket knife

3M 6000 series respirator w/organic prefilters

Safety glasses

Transparent water hose: 30 feet of ½-inch or ¾-inch (for water leveling hull)

Handsaw: Japanese dozuki with crosscut and rip blades

Scissors: 8- to 10-inch blades

Handheld propane torch with fuel cartridges

Miscellaneous screwdrivers

Sawhorses: at least two, 24 inches high

Surgical gloves: for working with epoxy

Prices of the above items approximately $650

Additional Tools and Materials

Waterless hand soap (e.g. Fast Orange): to remove epoxy, or automotive hand cleaner

Tongue depressors or stirring sticks

Autobody plastic squeegees: for spreading thickened epoxy

Disposable mixing cups: graduated 13- to 16-ounce, for mixing epoxy and hardener

or

Minipumps or gear pumps for dispensing and measuring epoxy and hardener

Steel baling wire: two rolls for wiring up hulls (If boat is over 16 feet, substitute 14-gauge electric fence wire.)

Sandpaper: 80-, 150-, and 220-grit
Shop vacuum (optional)
Pencils: two
Battens: ¾-inch x ¾-inch x 16 feet, and
   ½-inch x ½-inch x 10 feet
Router with ½- and ¼-inch carbide
   roundover bits (optional)
Parrot-peak wire-cutter pliers: Knipex
   KN6801, 8-inch

Advanced Tools

Bandsaw: 14-inch
Table saw: 10-inch
Wood planer: 12-inch, Makita #2012
   Power Feed with 12-amp motor
Disc belt sander: Delta 31-730 6 x 48-inch
   belt and 12-inch-disc finishing
   machine
Cutoff saw: 10-inch, Makita LS1030
Drill press: Delta 11-990 12-inch bench
   model
Air compressor

HVLP (high velocity, low pressure) spray
   gun for painting
Drawknife
Cordless drill: Panasonic EY6205BC 12-
   volt, heavy-duty, ½-inch, with keyless
   chuck
Orbital sander
Hand power plane: Makita #1900B
   (3½ inch)
Wood rasps
Plug cutters
Mechanic's wrenches
Sledgehammer: short-handled
Jointer: 6-inch or larger
Compressed air stapler: SENCO
   LN4450, drives ¼-inch wide crown
   staples, up to 1-inch long.
Shop workbench and vise
Cold chisel set
Punches and nail sets
Ball peen hammer

3

SELECTING
A SUITABLE DESIGN

If this is your first boatbuilding project, it is wise to begin with a small, simple boat. Building confidence and skill is more important than building the boat itself. Many boatbuilders have undertaken too large a project, only to stall out or totally abandon the effort. Materials can exceed $6 per pound of a boat's dry weight, and the weight of the boat increases exponentially with its length. Cost overruns can quickly and fatally affect the outcome of the project. Labor, too, increases exponentially with size. Build big if you must, but be sure to consider all the ramifications, including the additional equipment.

Once you have developed your boatbuilding skills on smaller boats, you can move on to bigger boats with confidence and a healthy dose of experience tucked away in your toolbox.

When selecting a boat design, consider whether the boat will be trailered, whether you will need winter storage, and where you will keep it during the summer months. Imagine how you'll use your boat, including your performance and comfort expectations. To understand the dynamics of a boat, study the hull form. Think of a

pendulum; the deeper the hull, the longer and slower the hull will swing. Conversely, the shallower the hull, the shorter and faster the swing. A boat's stability depends directly on the width and depth of its hull.

Don't scrimp on blueprints and the cost of plans, as this will certainly frustrate your results. A good set of plans is like a road map, guiding you step by step through your boatbuilding journey. Poor

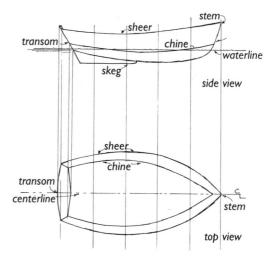

Figure 3-1. Basic parts of a V-bottomed boat.

plans will almost certainly assure that you'll lose your way. Look for a classical, clean design, one with what I refer to as a "boat-like" look. Try to avoid designs that attempt to make a silk purse from sows' ears or cram the accommodations of a 35-footer into a 25-foot hull.

Think carefully about how you will use the boat. Watch how boats move through the water; you'll become adept in the mental process of critiquing and discerning proper boat design. There should be a right feel about the design, even in your imagination. Whether a boat has conventional sheer or straight sheer, whether it has one shape or another, you can develop an educated sense about its balance and proportion. Learn to trust your instincts as your boat sense evolves, and help the process by reading magazines and books and by observing all types of boats on your waterways.

Boatbuilding can and should be a lifetime process, so it's never too late to get started. I started as a young boy, observing boats with my Dad at boat shows. We'd amble up and down the aisles, stopping only when a special boat would catch our eye and demand closer appraisal. My young and untutored eye would force me to stop and dwell on a boat that looked pleasing and just right to me. Soon, I could sense that certain "boat-like" look, and could imagine how a particular boat would move in the water, and why it might give its owner great satisfaction and pride.

I spent my childhood in Oregon's Willamette Valley, and there saw the wonderful McKenzie River drift boats and the graceful but rugged coastal dories. These boats were highly evolved for their purposes: fishing on whitewater rivers or punching over turbulent coastal surf to fish the Pacific. Although they had undergone many evolutionary changes, these boats were always built of plywood.

To my young eyes, these were beautiful shapes to behold. The drift boat had a strong sheer and extremely rockered bottom.

The coastal dories plied those treacherous waters, where the bays were accessible only by passage through rough surf and over dangerous sandbars. Heavily influenced by the drift boats, the dories were designed with extreme sheer and sufficient rise in the bow to tackle the rough surf and bar conditions. It dawned on me, at some early point, that rough water is unforgiving of eccentric design and poorly constructed boats. So the characteristics I sought from my earliest observations were great strength in the sheer and an overall design that would handle the roughest conditions.

Since those early years my designs have been a mix of self-induced and commissioned inspiration, ranging from 7-foot 6-inch dinghies to 42-foot sailboats and 43-foot powerboats. All are stitch-and-glue, and all share the common heritage of coming from my heart.

I'm often told that my boats are much different in real life from the way they look in their drawings, and I'm not sure whether that's an insult to my drafting or a compliment to the spirit of the boat. I'll hang on to the thought that it's a reflection of the boat's spirit, honestly earned through the inspiration of its designer and the labors of its builders. Any boat that's honest in its origin—sweated over, at times bled on, and often cursed at—can be one of the sweetest pieces of art going.

4

SELECTING MARINE PLYWOOD
AND DIMENSIONAL LUMBER

MARINE PLYWOOD

Since stitch-and-glue boats are built of plywood, you'll need to know what quality of plywood to buy, how to judge that quality to ensure a first-rate boat, and where to locate top grades. Look for *marine* plywood that meets the British 1088 standard or American "AA" rating. Do your looking at a marine lumberyard that offers accurate information, fair pricing, and a reputation for quality in both marine plywood and dimensional lumber. Very likely you'll have to order by phone; look for sources in the boatbuilding magazines and in the List of Suppliers in the appendix.

There can be no compromise: the plywood *must* be marine grade. Plywood meant for house construction is much more susceptible to water and structural degradation. Sooner or later, non-marine plywood will fail in some manner. You'll quickly spend the few dollars you've saved—and much more—when it's time to repair or replace the cheaper plywood.

The American system of grading ply-

wood uses letters to designate the panel type. An "AA" designation indicates that the panel's two outside faces are the best grade, or "A" quality. In American grades of marine panels, the interior plies must also meet certain criteria, such as the solidity of the veneers and uniformity of species. This is important, since domestic marine plywood veneers can have fir, larch, or hemlock in their interior layers. The fir and larch are desirable, but stay away from hemlock—it is neither stable nor durable enough for marine use.

I'm prejudiced toward foreign plywoods that meet at least the BS 1088 standard; the American grading system allows for too much in the way of defects and voids within the interior veneers. To put it simply, if you want your boat to last twenty years or more, you had better use imported marine plywood.

This issue of using imported marine plywood was not so easily resolved. In the early years of my boatbuilding career, I used a lot of domestic fir marine plywood. Often, on a cool morning while walking out to the shop, I would notice the dew on the sides of a boat that was being stored in the yard. Although most of the boat's side would be covered with dew, there would be several small, elliptical dry areas in a random pattern. They were shaped exactly like the repair patches I'd often noticed on the faces of the plywood. One day, I drilled a hole in one such dry area and discovered that, lo and behold, it was actually a void in the interior plies of the wood.

You can probably guess that it wasn't too easy to drill holes in each of the dry spots on that boat to inject epoxy into the voids. Yet, if these holes or voids aren't properly filled and sealed, you're just asking for moisture to work its way into the interior of the plywood and begin its dastardly work of swelling the wood fiber, delaminating the plies, and even permitting rot to set in.

You will pay for cheap plywood many times over. We once constructed two 19-foot Winter Wren Class sailboats side by side using the same epoxy, the same glass cloth, and the same work crew. One boat was built of less expensive fir marine plywood, the other of very expensive imported marine plywood from Holland. As it happened, both boats were launched the same day, and both came back to our shop for refinishing during the same summer season about four years later. Both were repainted, revarnished, and checked very carefully for any potential problems. The inexpensive fir plywood boat had only one defect, a gouge where the outboard engine, being raised out of the water, had hit the transom edge. The other boat showed no problems.

When both jobs were completed, I noticed something strange about the two work bills. The bill for the first boat, the Winter Wren built with the fir plywood,

indicated $46 more in materials cost and almost double the labor for its refit. The added material expense was in two areas, sandpaper and a small amount of epoxy, the latter used for the transom-edge fix. Why double the labor and why more sandpaper used in the job? Answer: the fir plywood was nowhere near as smooth and fair as the Dutch plywood, and it simply required more extensive sanding and preparation for repainting.

The owner of the boat built with the premium-grade plywood had spent an additional $900 for the Dutch plywood, but he saved more than $600 in labor for the first major refit of his boat. That savings, if you consider that he would refit at least every four years, would more than pay for the expensive plywood by the boat's sixth year. In addition, the beautiful grain of the more expensive plywood allowed me to varnish the whole interior of the boat, while the fir plywood boat had to be painted because of surface imperfections.

Of the imported marine plywoods, I commonly use three species of African mahogany—khaya, sapele, and okoume. All three are available in a variety of thicknesses and all are suitable for use in a marine environment. Hull panels, bulkheads, and decks can all be built with these plywoods. Okoume, which is a salmon-pink color, is the lightest in weight and the least strong of the mahoganies, but I often use it as the base of my stitch-and-glue hulls. Khaya and sapele are both a bit heavier and show up a much darker color when epoxy-sealed. Sapele's grain pattern is particularly beautiful and can make for spectacular brightwork when varnished.

Because quality stitch-and-glue boat construction depends on top-grade marine plywood, I often test plywood stock when it arrives at my shop (especially if it comes from a new or different manufacturer). I cut 4-inch squares from sample sheets and boil them for 20 to 30 minutes in a small pan. Then I take them directly from the boiling water and place them in the freezer. When they have frozen solid, I boil them again, repeating this cycle three times. If your plywood can withstand this test, it will probably last a long time.

You might also dry the test pieces in the oven to more closely simulate what will happen to plywood when it's part of a boat in service. Boats experience wild swings of temperature and undergo cycles of soaking and drying. They are trailered over hot highways, launched into cold water, then hauled and dried out once again. Keep this constant punishment in mind when you select your materials, especially the plywood.

Although epoxies are wonderful products that have made modern wooden boats an economical possibility, they aren't quite the miracle workers some people believe. An epoxy-sealed and encapsulated boat is only as good as the material it was built from. Epoxy cannot atone for an inherent weakness in the wood.

Checking—fine cracks in the face of the plywood—allows moisture to enter the plywood laminate. It is the greatest enemy of marine plywood and the biggest liability of plywood boat construction. Checking is most common in fir plywood, usually appearing as small cracks running lengthwise along the grain of the wood. Checking, and its attendant problems, may be the result of the plywood manufacturing process. Fir logs are thoroughly soaked and steamed before the veneering process, where rotary cutters peel the log's layers,

forcing its curved surfaces to suddenly lie flat. That stress may manifest itself later as cracks.

This checking problem can persist even through epoxy sealing and fiberglass/epoxy sheathing. Individual veneers and glue lines in the plywood may restrict the moisture problem to local areas, but even isolated areas are subject to swelling and contraction, and ultimately, to delamination and failure. It is persistent enough to almost convince me against ever using fir marine plywood in my boats.

One final comment about plywood. Rot requires three things to flourish. It must have a food source (which the wood eagerly supplies), oxygen (which is already present within the wood cells), and moisture. Moisture is the element most within our control. Lesser grades of plywood can have internal voids that can act like straws, drawing moisture to the interior. Any kind of break in the veneer, sealant, or sheathing—no matter how small—will act as a straw sucking in moisture from outside. While you are assembling your stitch-and-glue boat, vigilantly inspect the plywood edges for voids or empty spaces of any type. And always be sure to seal all plywood edges and surfaces with epoxy to ensure maximum longevity and help prevent moisture invasion and veneer degradation.

DIMENSIONAL LUMBER

There are many components on the stitch-and-glue boat that require dimensional (non-plywood) lumber—gunwales, skegs, keels, breasthooks, and seat thwarts, for example. A larger boat may call for dimensional lumber for sheer clamps, rubrails, sheerstrakes, bowsprits, masts, booms, deck beams, tillers, and cheekblocks.

There are two classifications for dry dimensional wood: *air-dried* and *kiln-dried*. It is imperative in any structure that will be encapsulated and sealed with epoxy (as in a stitch-and-glue boat) that all wood used be as dry as possible before sealing. Air-dried wood is usually better and easier to work with because the high temperatures of the kiln-drying process can rob the wood of suppleness and strength. You will find that the kiln-dried is harder and can be more brittle, a distinct disadvantage in boatbuilding. On the other hand, economics may dictate the use of kiln-dried, since it is usually less expensive, and more universally available than air-dried lumber.

Air-drying wood requires patience; the wood needs approximately one year per inch of thickness to dry fully. During this lengthy process, much care must be taken to avoid warping or cupping, and the wood must be constantly monitored to protect against invading insects. Most lumberyards simply don't trouble themselves with stocking air-dried woods.

Furthermore, small lumberyards tend not to have a good selection of exotic hardwoods, usually confining the bulk of their dimensional stock to domestic softwoods. While softwoods may be useful for certain parts of your boat, you will still need to find a source of hardwoods for other parts. Depending on your locale, you might have some excellent indigenous hardwoods, not to mention softwoods. Research the wood technology texts to find which local woods are durable and stable enough to make good boatbuilding materials. Here in the Northwest, we have a lot of Douglas fir (a softwood), which is stable, durable, and can be used for almost any part of the boat from keel to mast. The problem, though, is that most of the best clear, virgin-growth fir

is being exported to foreign markets as fast as it can be logged.

Investigate the boatbuilding magazines for lumberyards that specialize in boatbuilding woods. Indeed, these yards may be your best bet, since turning to an expert is always the way to avoid confusion and eliminate the costly errors of using the wrong type or grade of wood. Any lumber dealer that advertises in a national magazine sells mail-order.

Always look for clear-grained wood, because knots and defects create untold problems. Often, dimensional wood stock will be bright finished (varnished) and visible on the finished boat. Clear stock will make your building job much easier, and will result in less waste.

Especially if it is kiln-dried, look for lengthwise cracks and for any discoloring, which might indicate incipient decay. When you're buying mail-order, be specific as to your expectations. When you want clear stock, make sure the order-taker understands this.

Be sure to note the grain of the wood—flat, vertical, or mixed. "Flat grain"

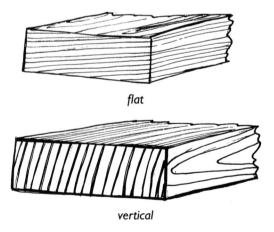

flat

vertical

Figure 4-1. Wood grains.

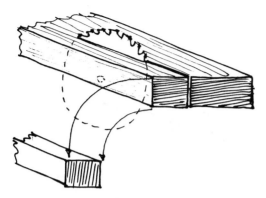

Figure 4-2. Cutting a flat-grained board to produce vertical-grained pieces.

means that the grain lines are parallel to the wide face of the board. In a vertically grained board the grain lines are perpendicular to the wide face. In dimensional lumber of square cross section, you can convert flat grain to vertical simply by rotating the piece 90 degrees. If you are bending gunwales with a cross section of ¾ x 1½ inches on a small boat, a gunwale with a vertical grain will be harder to bend, but stiffer and stronger. A flat- or mixed-grain gunwale would bend easier, but won't be nearly as strong. And, when making a sheer clamp on a larger boat, where multiple layers of dimensional wood must be laminated to form the clamp, flat-grained wood will bend into place more readily, fasten easier, and do so without as much splitting.

In the grand old-growth forests of our great-grandfathers' times the trees were cut eight to ten feet from the ground to avoid the burls, butt growth, and other irregularities at their bases. Often there was twisted grain at the base due to weight compression and other natural causes, and builders realized early on that when this wood at the base was dried, it tended to crack, twist, and warp. But big trees were plentiful, so they simply ignored the bottom of the log. Today, loggers cut as flush to the ground as possible to maximize tree footage, and butt- or twisted-grain woods often end up in lumberyard stock.

To detect grain problems, sight the length of the board, and if the grain slants out to the edge of the piece, you have grain runout. If it is pronounced, you can assume it is from a butt-cut log and it may be a very unstable piece of wood. Once glued into the boat these pieces will be more prone to cracks and joint failures that can be nearly impossible to repair. Use the same criteria for selecting dimensional lumber as you use for selecting marine plywood: Look for quality, accurate lumberyard information, and fair pricing, but expect to pay a goodly amount for good stock.

Wood Types

Douglas Fir. Readily available, fir is light in color with a slightly reddish tone and a long, straight grain. It is light in weight relative to its strength. For our purposes, it takes a fine finish and can be easily glued. You will find fir the best wood for keels, stringers, and clamps. It is also suitable for masts and spars.

Spruce. There are still vast forests of clear, old-growth spruce being harvested, especially in Canada and Alaska—most notably, Sitka spruce. Spruce is absolutely the best wood for masts, booms, gaffs, and bowsprits. The major advantages of spruce are its light weight and extreme inter-grain strength. Spruce's blond color is similar to Douglas fir but not as reddish. When epoxy-sealed, spruce tends to yellow quite a bit.

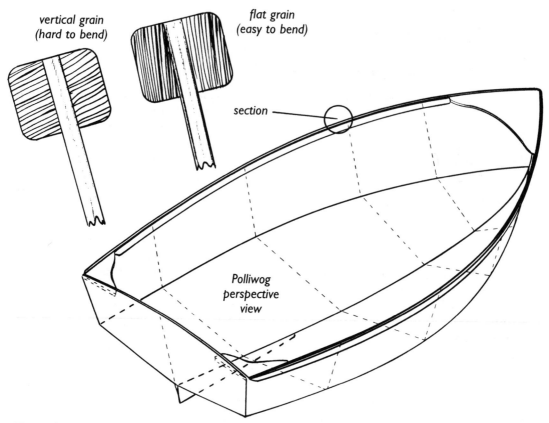

vertical grain
(hard to bend)

flat grain
(easy to bend)

section

Polliwog
perspective
view

Figure 4-3. Bending wood into a sheer clamp.

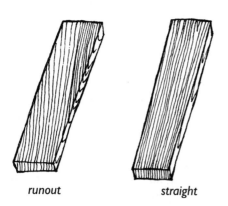

runout   straight

*Figure 4-4. Grain runout, left, may indicate
an unstable piece of lumber.*

For consistency of color, you must take great care to seal the wood evenly.

For spars, you will need long, straight-grained pieces of spruce, preferably air-dried. If you use kiln-dried spruce, check that the drying was consistent and the wood is uniform in dryness and appearance. If you foresee that your building project will stretch over a long period, buy partially air-dried or green wood and carefully regulate its final drying, allowing the wood to stabilize while the building project is underway.

Mahogany. Mahogany is used extensively in boatbuilding. The best available to us these days is Honduras mahogany from Central America. A durable, beautiful hardwood with dark red color and a distinctive grain that takes a bright, clear finish, mahogany will never frustrate you. It glues superbly, seals well, and is always worth its premium price.

Also worth considering are the darker African khaya mahogany, and okoume, a salmon-pink mahogany that is also from Africa. Khaya and okoume are the main species used for high-grade European marine plywood.

Lauan mahogany (and its relatives) is available in a range of colors from red to pink. It is technically not a true mahogany but is more closely related to the cedar family. Its grain is quite fine and it works wonderfully with hand tools. In the U.S. market, lumberyards usually stock lauan from the Philippines or Indonesia. This mahogany is recognizable by its speckled grain with a base color of reddish brown. Use the darker, denser varieties. There is also a subspecies of lauan mahogany called meranti—the most durable lauan available.

Watch for wind shakes or jagged lines and cracks across the grain, in lauans especially. These defects can be traced to logging practices that allow trees to fall over each other, and to clear-cutting, which eliminates protection from extreme tropical storms. It's easy to miss these defects until the piece has been milled and is in place on the boat, so watch carefully.

Teak. Teak is a great wood for exterior surfaces, particularly rubrails, sheer guards, handrails, toerails, decks, and seat thwarts. Teak is heavy and durable and will withstand more abuse and neglect than almost any other wood. It is a dark chocolate-brown wood, with a beautiful and pro-

nounced grain. I never use anything but teak for toerails and rubrails, and these parts rarely get an epoxy-sealed and varnished finish on my boats. Instead, I apply several coats of teak oil annually, after a scrubbing to remove mold or moss growth. If the toerail or rubrail is damaged slightly, the oil finish allows me to smooth out the damage with a block plane and a bit of sandpaper. A light coat of teak oil restores the finish without missing a beat.

A fairly recent arrival on the market is Cetol, a teak finish by the Sikkens Company that you apply much like a varnish. Its color on the first application is sort of a startling orange, but it blends well with the teak's natural color after a couple of coats. Cetol is durable, and easy to touch-up and maintain—important concerns in my shop.

Though teak is very forgiving as well as handsome and workable, no wood is maintenance-free. In the Northwest I see altogether too many neglected teak surfaces on boats, which take on a silvery appearance and often a growth of green moss. It's so simple to scrub teak with a mild bleach and water solution that there is really no excuse for ignoring it as much as often happens.

In the interior, you might use teak for trim, the fiddles, cleat stock, and the floorboards. Because it is dark, however, teak is easy to overuse. Too much teak makes a dank and somber interior, and will quickly add a lot of weight to the boat. Its greatest drawback, however, is that it simply does not glue well. When you fasten teak, prepare adjoining surfaces for snug fits and wipe down with acetone and a clean rag to remove the natural oils before applying epoxy glues or polysulfide adhesives such as Sikaflex or 3M 5200. Then, when you mate the surfaces, use plenty of mechanical fasteners such as screws or bolts.

Yellow Cedar. Two species of yellow cedar are popular boatbuilding woods. Both are lightweight and have good strength. These woods hold mechanical fasteners well and have excellent durability. My preference is Port Orford cedar. A native of the Northwest, it has a honey-blond color and a sweet, pungent smell that I never tire of while working it. Durable and rot-resistant, it glues well, takes a finish readily, and like fir, has many uses. Virtually any part of the boat could be built from Port Orford cedar. In boatbuilding heaven, I'd make boats of Port Orford cedar plywood.

Alaskan yellow cedar has similar qualities but its aroma is more pungent, often reminding me of juniper berries. Both Port Orford and Alaskan yellow cedar are members of the cypress family and have all the desirable characteristics of cypress: durability, good gluing ability, and high strength-to-weight ratios.

Oak. White oak is a hardwood that runs beige to nut-brown in color. It is medium to heavy in weight, has high strength, and is potentially durable—though sometimes I have seen this wood rot with frightening speed. I think its tendency to rot may be related to the season of harvest. Oak harvested during the spring, when the sap is flowing at its maximum, seems to have a much greater tendency to rot. If the tree is harvested in the fall or winter, when the sap is down, I would wager that the wood might last forever.

White oak is used in areas of the boat where extreme strength is needed. Gunwale clamps and rubrails are the two most usual places. I favor this wood for tillers, which need to be as strong as possible. The glueability of white oak has been questioned, but I have never had any trouble. As with teak, it's best to wipe down white oak with acetone and a clean rag before gluing, and mechanical fasteners should be used to assist the bond to other surfaces.

Red oak possesses many of the same physical characteristics as white oak—although it isn't as durable—and has the same kinds of uses on a boat. It has a higher cell porosity and is thus more penetrable by liquid than white oak, so it may be somewhat more susceptible to decay.

There is an old adage I keep in mind when selecting oak. *When examining a pile, if you find even one piece of wood with rot in it, avoid the lot!*

Specialty Woods. Specialty woods may be used on any boat, particularly to decorate and to highlight customized interior work. My advice is to limit the variety of woods, using no more than four or five types per boat, and always consider how well the wood will glue; if you are in doubt be sure to add mechanical fasteners.

Along with the finest grades of imported marine plywood, I prefer fir gunwales and clamps, Honduras mahogany floor timbers, deck beams, and interior trim, spruce spars, oak for tillers, and teak for exterior guards and trim. My concern for design simplicity leads me to caution against too many different woods: Simple is often better. And for heaven's sake, don't fool with the natural color of the wood. Staining diminishes the wood's ability to seal with epoxy, and the natural color God gave the wood is always the best one.

5

EPOXY SYSTEMS

EPOXY RESIN AND HARDENER

While stitch-and-glue boat construction was possible before epoxy, the development of these adhesives has made possible the building of larger boats of much higher quality and greater strength. Before epoxy, the reinforced joints had to be made with layers of fiberglass cloth and polyester resin. Most of the boats made with polyester resins were dinghy-sized and had to be taken out of the water when not in use. The bonding characteristics of the polyester resin was limited greatly by the skills of the builder, and the durability of the boat depended heavily on proper maintenance. If those early boats were left to soak or were abused, the plywood quickly absorbed water and swelled. When dried out, the wood shrank, and after a lot of those cycles the resins would release their bond to the wood—and as a consequence, many early boats suffered from resin/cloth failures.

When epoxy use in boat construction came onto the scene in the 1970s, its greater strength and durability opened a wide range of new possibilities. Boats could be made much larger. They could be left in the water without fear of absorbing water, and a stitch-and-glue boat's life expectancy increased tremendously. Concerns for maintenance were greatly reduced, while structural integrity was greatly enhanced.

Epoxy is a multipurpose material for boatbuilding. It is used as a coating to seal all of the plywood and dimensional wood surfaces, and as a glue for the structural joints. It can be mixed with wood flour or other fillers to make strong structural fillets. Epoxy is also used with fiberglass cloth to reinforce seams and sheathe exterior surfaces, giving us a strong waterproof structure.

Because of its chemical makeup, epoxy offers distinct advantages to polyester resin. First, it is a much stronger adhesive. Second, it has far superior secondary bonding characteristics (the ability to stick to wood or a previously cured epoxy or polyester surface). And third, it is a superior moisture barrier.

On the down side, epoxy requires greater precision when mixing the resin and hardener, it can be toxic if improperly used, and lastly, it is more expensive.

Epoxy is a two-part adhesive. The resin component is a clear, syrupy liquid, while the hardener is thicker (more viscous) and usually the color of honey. These liquid resins and hardeners must be mixed using the exact ratio specified by the manufacturer. This ratio will differ greatly from one system to another, so be sure to follow the manufacturer's directions precisely. Beware that a deviation of as little as five percent in either direction can undermine the final physical properties of the cured epoxy. And once you have mixed the liquids in the correct ratio, they must be fully and thoroughly stirred, scraping the surfaces of the mixing container and moving all the liquids around until you are sure of a complete blend.

When mixed, the epoxy undergoes an exothermic reaction, generating heat as it cures. As this reaction occurs, the liquid thickens and becomes a solid. Ambient air temperature affects the speed with which the epoxy sets up, or, as I say in my shop, *goes off*. The optimal temperature for epoxy is around 75°F. The lower the temperature, the slower the cure.

To counter this effect, epoxy manufacturers formulate various "speeds" of hardeners. In the Northwest, where temperatures stay fairly moderate, I use a fast hardener through most of the year, switching to a slower formulation in the two or three warmest months. The resin formulation for boatbuilding is always the same; only the hardener component varies. If you should choose to use a fast hardener on days above 80°F, be prepared to work fast and mix small batches.

It is not uncommon to have a container of epoxy smoke or even "flash off."

When a batch of epoxy overheats in your container, remove it from your workspace immediately. Use caution: The epoxy can become hot enough to melt the plastic mixing container! And don't breathe the fumes if the epoxy has begun to flash.

If I find the epoxy flashing off, or boiling, I mix smaller amounts or switch to a slower hardener. Pouring the batch into a larger, flat container can help dissipate heat and slow the rate of cure also.

Under average conditions, the epoxy takes 24 hours to reach an easily sandable state, but again, this varies with temperature. In the summer, when temperatures range between 80° and 90°F, I have been able to epoxy a small project in the morning and then work with it in the afternoon. In the winter months, when the temperature hovers around 40° to 45°F, an epoxied surface can remain slightly tacky even after 24 hours.

You must be patient with epoxy when working in an unheated space. Space heaters are not always the solution. I have used a kerosene space heater to warm the shop and accelerate the rate of cure, but found, to my dismay, that the incomplete combustion of the kerosene leaves a minute residue in the air that can foul the material surfaces, interfering with the epoxy's ability to bond. Both propane and natural gas space heaters have similar problems also, creating water as a byproduct of combustion. If you are tempted to use space heaters, use electric quartz heaters. These infrared heaters do not heat the air, rather they heat the surfaces of the objects the infrared waves encounter. You can find quartz space heaters at most industrial equipment suppliers.

None of the suppliers of boatbuilding epoxies actually manufactures their own

Figure 5-1. Mixing epoxy in a graduated cup, right, is an accurate alternative to an expensive epoxy dispenser.

raw resins and hardeners. Each supplier formulates its resins and hardeners by mixing base stock material with various additives that vary the epoxy's properties and performance.

As a very rough rule of thumb, the greater the proportion of resin to hardener, the harder the cured epoxy will be. For example, epoxies that use two parts resin to one part hardener are generally more flexible than those using five parts resin to one part hardener. If you are confused by suppliers' claims as to the physical properties of their systems, I recommend you experiment on your own. Try to settle on one system that will meet all your needs. Consider product availability. Select an epoxy manufacturer who supplies adequate technical manuals; the more specific the manual, the better. Some formulators have gone to the additional step of demonstrating how to use their products in specific boatbuilding applications, and maintain a staff of experienced technicians for telephone assistance. A high level of service is a distinct advantage.

Since the epoxy is the most critical component, it's important that you not allow cost to prevent you from buying the best available. Most of the failures of boatbuilding epoxies have been with cheap systems. The better epoxy systems come from reputable companies that have their own research staff constantly testing to ensure a high-quality product.

Once you have chosen a suitable epoxy system, you must be able to measure the resin and hardener in the exact ratios. I prefer using graduated cups, but when you get into the five-to-one systems, the use of cups can be complicated. Still, for shop purposes, I use graduated cups for small batches, and if I want larger batches, I measure with graduated cups into a bucket for mixing.

Some systems use precalibrated pumps that mount on the resin and hardener cans. One pump stroke from the resin can, and one from the hardener can, delivers the proper mixing ratio.

Mechanical gear pumps are also available for high-volume dispensing of the correct ratio of resin to hardener. The purchase cost of these pumps might be considerable, but as with all tools, don't scrimp; the correct pump will speed the construction process, help minimize waste, and deliver more accurate resin-to-hardener ratios.

All measuring devices must be kept clean to function properly. They will tend to gunk up, collect dust, and build up residue until they simply won't serve their intended purpose accurately. During his annual visit to my shop, the local fire marshal always comments that these buildups on dispensers are a fire hazard, and no amount of arguing seems to dissuade him. From that point of view graduated cups work best because they get thrown out when past their prime.

I routinely check the epoxy work of the previous day when I open the shop in the morning. If a surface seems too tacky or not properly cured, the culprit is almost always improper mixing. A quick check of the dispensers or the plunger openings usually proves me right. Colder shop temperatures will make the epoxy more viscous, which can affect the accuracy of the metering system. If the dispenser is clogged, use chemical-proof gloves with long, sleeve-covering gauntlets to clean all the parts with solvent. Before reassembling, lubricate the moving parts that won't have physical contact with the epoxy.

After the plungers are fully reloaded with the liquid, use a measuring cup or a weight scale to be sure that the correct amount of resin or hardener is being dispensed. Sounds easy enough, but cleaning these dispensers is messy work.

SAFETY

The most controversial aspect of epoxy use is the matter of safety. Stitch-and-glue boatbuilding relies on epoxy to ensure the strength and integrity of the seams and to seal all plywood surfaces. Because epoxy plays such a key role, it's important to have a clear understanding of this group of chemicals. There is no way around it: *The improper use of epoxy can be injurious and hazardous to your health.* But I think that constant vigilance and continuous care for safe and proper use will minimize the hazard. Boatbuilders using normal precautions and staying safety-minded at all times can use epoxy with the best of results while fully protecting their health.

The strongest advice I can give you is to keep epoxy off your skin. Prolonged contact with the resin and hardener can cause an allergic reaction—sensitization—in some people. Once sensitized, the slightest contact with the resin and hardener, their fumes, or even sanding dust from epoxy that hasn't fully cured can bring on a reaction.

Keep epoxy off your tools, and always wear gloves that protect wrists as well as hands. I know of three examples where boatbuilders threw caution to the wind and suffered the consequences. Two were first-time builders of boats, but one was a professional who should have known better. The common denominator was failure to use proper gloves. The professional was

a reckless fool in all aspects of his life. He refused to use gloves and would plunge his hands into acetone at the end of each job to clean off half-cured resin. While using urethane paints, he would refuse to wear even the simplest dust-filter mask, let alone an organic-vapor respirator or even a fresh-air system. Predictably, he experienced lung damage from the urethane paint and spent several days spitting up blood. In addition, the exposure to the epoxy caused a rash on both wrists and his

Figure 5-2. Using a glassing box to saturate sections of interior glass taping laminates. Note the large paper tub, top, used to hold larger amounts of mixed epoxy. The worker is using a squeegee to help spread the resin into the glass cloth; gloves, a Tyvek suit, and a canister respirator complete the outfit.

forehead that resembled a reaction to poison oak. The rash would disappear after five or six days if he stayed clear of epoxy, but as soon as he walked back into the shop, it reappeared. In the end, he had to give up boatbuilding with epoxy altogether, and the last I heard of him, he was at work in a can factory.

When I consulted with the two amateur builders, we traced their reactions to the cleanup process. Most gloves available to boatbuilders are adequate for epoxy but will never stand up to cleanup solvents such as acetone or lacquer thinner. The fingertips are weak, and after normal use, the solvents can easily leak through to the skin. In both cases, I found that uncured epoxy had repeatedly been allowed to stay in contact with the builders' hands. Over time, they each experienced increased skin sensitization. When cleaning up, discard the thin latex gloves you used for epoxying and don heavy, solvent-proof gloves.

And then there's "Devlin's Law," a variant of Murphy's Law. After a goodly amount of experience I have identified three natural temptations that you will experience when you are working with epoxy. *Once you have epoxy on your gloves, you WILL have an itch on your nose, your eyes WILL need to be rubbed, and you WILL begin to sweat and need to wipe your brow.* I guarantee you'll experience these urges, and just as surely, if you succumb to temptations, you will experience some nose or eye sensitization due to epoxy exposure.

There is simply no alternative to constant vigilance: using safety gear, working as cleanly as possible, and not getting epoxy on your skin. Keeping Devlin's Law in mind, one reason for wearing a canister respirator—apart from the fumes and dust—is to keep yourself from scratching

your nose. After fifteen years of using epoxies almost daily, the only reaction I notice is a slight constriction of the throat during extended use. But when I use a respirator, I never experience the throat irritation.

Of the two epoxy components, the hardener is the most toxic. Keep this in mind, particularly when cleaning the hardener side of your epoxy dispenser. Extreme caution should also be used when sanding partially cured (green) epoxy surfaces, as may happen in the winter in an unheated shop. Always wear a respirator and protective clothing, even if it's only street clothes that are laundered daily and cover all parts of the body likely to come in contact with uncured epoxy. If you insist on keeping your beard, a full-hood, powered-respirator fresh-air system may be the only answer, since regular cartridge-type respirators will not seal properly over a beard.

The bottom line, my macho friends, is to respect these chemicals; just because the hazards are invisible does not mean they are absent. If you are apt to disregard such hazards, and won't adopt a fervent attitude about safety, build your boat using traditional methods and stay away from stitch-and-glue construction.

I have seen a couple instances of almost magical acts of reverse gravity in which epoxy or its resin and hardener components splashed *up* into a boatbuilder's eyes. In each instance we had to rush the victim outside to a water hose for a lengthy flushing of his eyes, then rush him to the emergency room where the doctor repeated the process—not something anyone would do by choice. Wear eye protection at all times. Safety glasses don't work well for me because I find them uncomfortable. And if eyeglasses are uncomfortable, at some point you'll find yourself working without them—and that's when accidents happen. Even if you don't wear eyeglasses for vision, get yourself fitted with a proper expensive set of frames with clear lenses. Spend some money on them so you won't treat them casually and wreck them. Then wear them constantly in the shop so you get used to them.

And even the protection can't be taken for granted. I've also seen a worker develop nasty-looking, painful hands as a reaction to latex disposable gloves, which in his case was probably a reaction to the talcum powder in them. He was fine after he switched to non-talc gloves over soft lightweight cotton liner gloves.

Moderation is the best protection. Always shower after a work session; it will help keep your body clean and healthy. Also don't forget to launder your clothing often. Wearing the epoxy-encrusted clothes day after day just continues to expose yourself to uncured resin or hardener.

BASIC EPOXY TIPS

I always try to use the hottest (fastest-curing) hardener, taking into account the weather and temperature. Some epoxy systems now provide custom blends for specific weather conditions, but even on the hottest days of the year, I have found that simple trial-and-error experimentation with a couple of slower hardeners helps me identify the appropriate hardener for that day. Keep records for future reference of which combinations work best under specific weather conditions in your area.

It is also important to store the resin and hardener at a consistent temperature, especially during the winter months. The better you control the epoxy's tempera-

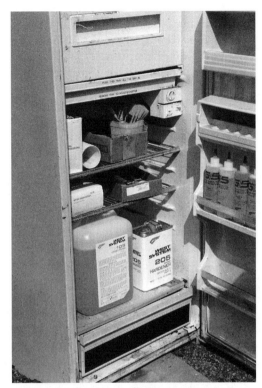

Figure 5-3. A used refrigerator is great for storing of epoxy resin, hardener, graduated cups, stir sticks, chip brushes, and disposable gloves. For winter storage, a small 75- or 100-watt lightbulb will keep the contents nice and warm for easier use.

ture, the surer and more consistent the cure rates will be.

A way to keep the resin and hardener at a uniform temperature is to store the dispensers in a heated box. In my shop we use old refrigerators with 100-watt light bulbs for heat. With the compressor off and the light bulb on, the sealed interior stays at about 80°F. The freezer compartment also makes a handy place to store gloves, stir sticks, mixing cups, fillet squeegees and other epoxying paraphernalia. Of course, make sure that the refrigerator door is secure from inquisitive children.

As mentioned, mass also affects the rate at which the epoxy kicks off. The smaller, more confined, and narrower-mouthed the mixing container, the hotter the exothermic reaction and the faster the epoxy will go off. Consider transferring the epoxy into a larger flat-bottomed tub or tray to slow down the exothermic reaction and extend your working time.

Thin coats of epoxy applied with a roller or squeegee take more time to cure than thicker applications such as a taped epoxy-and-fiberglass hull seam, because the heat dissipates easily from a thin coating. When clear-coating panels of plywood with epoxy, you can apply an external heat source such as a heat gun or heat lamp to warm the entire coated surface. This will also help level the epoxy coating (helps to flow out) so that your surfaces are smoother and require less labor to prepare for paints or varnishes. Use caution, however, when applying heat to the first coat of epoxy on a dry wood surface. It's quite easy to lower the viscosity of the epoxy sufficiently to drive a small amount of it into the wood grain. While this doesn't compromise the sealing process, it may create finishing problems, because the thin epoxy can displace air bubbles (out-gassing) from the wood grain, causing the epoxy to cure with a pocked surface and necessitating another sealing coat. You can avoid this with a slight and very even application of heat.

Epoxy also seems to magically appear on every tool, clamp, and boatbuilding device in the shop. Epoxy crud can rear its ugly head anywhere. Its appearance may not bother you initially, but soon this residue will diminish the usefulness or precision of your tools. That's why it's important to clean up after each job. Epoxy

removers are available from most manufacturers, and solvents such as acetone and lacquer thinner will work well, too, on partially cured resin. Use long-sleeved, solvent-proof gloves when working with these solvents, since any skin contact will strip away your skin oils, which are your first line of protection. If a tool depends on lubrication, you will need to relubricate it after each cleaning with solvent. I have experimented with a number of different lubricants and have found that light oils such as WD-40 work best on tools that might be fouled by epoxy. Do not use epoxy solvents on tools such as hammers: The solvent might loosen the glues used to assemble the tool, and you certainly don't want to see hammer heads flying around the shop. Wipe off what you can, but it is better to clean these tools by sanding or chiseling off the epoxy crud after it has cured.

A suitable natural cleaner for uncured epoxy resins is white vinegar. Soaking the fouled tool or object in the vinegar will cause the epoxy resin to turn milky white and thick and eventually roll off the tool. Rinse with clean water and dry. You could also use vinegar to clean hands of uncured epoxy, but then you shouldn't be finding yourself in that position anyway.

The frustration of keeping a clean shop is experienced by everyone who works with epoxy. On a recent trip, I had a chance to visit the boatbuilding shop of the Gougeon Brothers in Bay City, Michigan. From their excellent book, *The Gougeon Brothers on Boat Construction*, I gathered they had solved the problems of keeping a tidy shop, and I wanted to see how they had done it. I found a well-organized shop and a crew with excellent work habits; but, like me, they haven't found a foolproof way to work with epoxy and keep everything clean. If one works under the pressure of deadlines, it will always be frustrating to work cleanly with epoxy, but try!

FILLERS

Fillers are used to modify epoxy for various applications, from fairing compounds to structural adhesives. Fillers are always added after the proper resin/hardener mixture has been thoroughly blended. You'll find a great variety of epoxy fillers on the market, including specialized formulations for everything from high-strength hardware bonding, to easy-sanding fillers. They are all quite expensive. I am of the opinion that a great variety is unnecessary. I have found that I need only three basic fillers: wood flour, Cabosil, and microballoons. These fillers adequately answer a variety of boatbuilding needs, and help to keep the overall material cost of the hull down. I might have just a small amount of high-density filler on hand for some hardware bonding purposes but the major players are wood flour, Cabosil, and microballoons.

Wood Flour

Wood flour fits the bill for stitch-and-glue boatbuilding because it is inexpensive and creates exceptionally strong joints. It is both a bulking and thixotropic filler, which means it will make a thickened epoxy that tools easily into joints but also stays in place once you've finished the application. Wood flour is little more than the finely ground sawdust commonly used in the baking industry as a cellulose filler for breads (fiber additive, if you must know) and in the manufacture of wood putties for home construction and cabinetry. It is finer than the sawdust made by your table saw or belt sander. Here in the Northwest, wood flour is listed in the Yellow Pages, and I usually buy it in 50-pound bags. It is also available from most epoxy suppliers. If it's not, yell and they will soon develop a supply of it.

Wood flour mixes uniformly with epoxy, making a thick paste. In my shop, we keep adding until the shininess of the epoxy has disappeared and the mixture looks like thick, creamy peanut butter. I use this paste to create the base for our stitch-and-glue composite seam wherever plywood sheets meet in the hull structure, and to cove (fillet) the joints for all permanent interior structures. Whenever I attach a cleat or shelf, I use the paste on the facing surfaces to glue the components in place.

By its nature, wood flour is the perfect partner to join plywood panels and the wood components of the boat because it shares the same cellulose composition and provides a close color match. I find it disconcerting to see a well-built boat with purple microballoons or white microspheres glaring out from every seam. If you plan to finish your interior bright, wood flour is the only way to go.

You might ask, as many do, "Why use a filler at all?" The answer is simple. It's nearly impossible to cut all components for a perfect fit, and there will be slight gaps between the surfaces being bonded together. Clear epoxy may run out of the joints or fail to fill the gaps and voids. Thickened epoxy will eliminate both problems while creating a joint that is actually stronger than the pieces being joined. If your joinery is perfect then by all means show it as such, but you can create a fine-looking boat with structural fillets that's probably stronger to boot.

Cabosil

Cabosil is a white powder that is used primarily as a thixotropic additive. It helps prevent epoxy from sagging on vertical surfaces, and it can enable you to apply a thicker sealer coating of epoxy in a single pass where unthickened epoxy might require several coats to achieve the same depth. I also mix Cabosil with wood flour to achieve a smooth, thick fillet on a vertical surface; it's not colored enough to take away from wood flour's natural color. Cabosil is a versatile filler that can be combined with other fillers to create custom blends tailored to a specific task.

Microballoons

When filling low spots with a thickened epoxy fairing compound in preparation for the final painting of the boat, wood flour has a couple of drawbacks. First, it doesn't sand easily, and its density is greater than necessary for a simple filling/fairing operation. In such cases I prefer an easier-to-sand compound made with epoxy and microballoons. Microballoons are lightweight phenolic spheres, light purple in color, and when mixed with epoxy, they make a dark purple filler that is easy to sand and sculpt. I think its color is unsightly and distracting in boat interiors unless the surface is painted, but I do like its ability to hold a feathered edge when sanded and to fill an unfair surface more rapidly than a wood flour mixture.

Finally, there is one additional filler that can be a real time-saver. Gougeon's West System 410 Microlight fairing compound is 30% easier to sand than microballoons, mixes into the epoxy faster, and has a tan color similar to wood flour's natural color. Since it's less dense and easier to sand than microballoons, many builders do most of their fairing with Microlight. It's more expensive, but it sure saves sanding and fairing time. Just make sure after using Microlight to reseal the surface with epoxy to help eliminate any difference in porosity (which would foul a paint job quickly).

6

FIBERGLASS CLOTH AND TAPE

Fiberglass fabric is an important part of the stitch-and-glue construction method. It is used to reinforce epoxied and filleted joints, sheathe exterior surfaces of the boat, and reinforce panels. Fiberglass/epoxy laminate helps exclude moisture and provides additional abrasion-resistance. It significantly improves the final strength and appearance of the stitch-and-glue boat, and without it, the integrity of an epoxied boat would be greatly compromised.

Fiberglass comes in various forms for boatbuilding, including woven and knitted cloths, and a random-fiber mat that resembles a coarse felt. Two are used extensively for stitch-and-glue construction. The woven cloth (and for our purposes in this book, any woven fiberglass fabric is a cloth) is particularly suited for use over composite joints (i.e., any joint reinforced with resin, fabric, and a fillet material) in small boats. But when building larger boats in which greater stresses will come to bear on the joints, the knitted biaxial fabrics are needed in tandem with the woven cloth to create strong, layered seams. In all stitch-and-glue boats the strong epoxy/fiberglass composite joints

replace the chine logs and frames of a traditional plywood boat.

To understand how fiberglass makes a boat's joints stronger, the builder must understand how the fabric is constructed. Fiberglass is made from continuous filaments of polyester glass, which are drawn or pulled from molten glass through precise, multiholed bushings. These filaments are combined into strands. Depending on the type of fiberglass, there may be from 51 to

Figure 6-1. Three types of fiberglass cloth used in stitch-and-glue boatbuilding: 6-ounce cloth, upper left corner; biaxial cloth, upper right; and peel-ply, bottom, used to make smoother laminates and ease sanding.

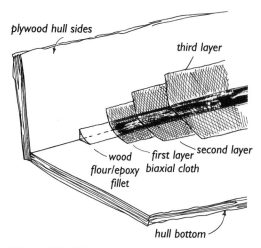

Figure 6-2. Fiberglass cloth tape overlaps at the chine joint.

1,224 filaments per strand. Thinner strands are called threads, and thicker strands with more filaments are yarns. Fiberglass is available in a variety of forms and will be characterized by the following properties: the number of yarns per inch in each direction, the weight of the fabric in ounces per square yard, the thickness in thousandths of an inch (mils), yarn construction, weave style, and finish. Most fiberglass fabrics are coated with lubricants so that the filaments won't fly away during the high-speed weaving process, and to ensure a uniform appearance. After the weaving is done, the fabric is heat-cleaned to remove most of the lubricant. Unfortunately, the heat also greatly reduces the tensile strength of the strands. All woven fiberglass products share this problem; if the strands need to be woven, lubricant is required, but the heat used to remove the lubricant diminishes the fiber strength.

It was only a matter of time (years actually) until someone asked, "Why weave it?" Consequently, the new developments in fiberglass technology switched from woven to knitted fabrics, which for our purposes mean biaxials and triaxials. Knitting machines easily handle the glass yarns without lubricants. The greatest boon to us, besides maintaining the original tensile strength, is that knitted fabrics can orient the fibers at 45° if desired, rather than only 90° as with woven fabric. With this orientation, more of the fabric crosses the joint, giving it immeasurably greater strength.

Knitted fabrics are rougher in texture than woven fabrics; if used alone, they don't finish nearly as smoothly as the woven cloth. The usual solution in stitch-and-glue construction is to use a woven cloth as the final surface layer over the knitted layers. For the interior seams of a stitch-and-glue boat multiple layers of knitted cloth covered with a layer of fiberglass tape significantly speed up the glassing of the hull and bulkhead seams. But when it comes to fiberglassing the upper portions of the boat—the more visible areas and places where you might want a more translucent or bright finish—biaxial or knitted fabrics are unsuitable, and the cloth tapes make for a more sightly joint.

Steer clear of premade woven fiberglass tapes, because their finish sizing reduces the wet-out capability of the epoxy, and the woven edges will tend to cause puckers in the middle of the tape. When applied over interior joints, these tapes do not flex or conform as well to the different angles and shapes of a boat. It is far more economical to cut your own widths of fiberglass tape from the standard 50-inch-wide, 6- or 8-ounce cloth woven material used for exterior sheathing of the hull. Unroll a length of the woven fiberglass cloth on a table and use a straightedge and a sharp knife—I like to use a single-sided razor

Figure 6-3. Cutting fiberglass cloth tapes from a roll of 6-ounce cloth with a safety razorblade and a straightedge. A slightly diagonal cut to the weave eliminates some of the unraveling.

blade—to cut strips at an angle of about 20 degrees to the weave. This helps keep the edges from unraveling during handling, and helps the tape conform to the joints.

When designing a stitch-and-glue boat, I examine each seam and joint for the level of stress it will experience to determine the number of layers of fiberglass or the amount of filleting that must be done. The higher the stress, the more layers of fiberglass tape necessary for adequate strength. The thickest seams will be in the interior main hull joints, the major bulkhead attachments, and the cabin and cockpit flats. These usually require two or three layers of tape—each one wider than the one before so that each bonds in part directly to the wood, and the joint is tapered. In boats larger than dinghies or skiffs I use layers of biaxial fiberglass tape, along with a woven fiberglass finish layer to smooth the joint.

The exterior fiberglass/epoxy sheathing serves two functions: It helps maintain a matrix of epoxy sealing that would otherwise be hard to regulate, and it adds considerable abrasion resistance. Local areas prone to abrasion can be further reinforced with additional layers of fiberglass cloth. A good example might be an extra layer of cloth on the foredeck where the anchor might someday be accidentally dropped, or on the forefoot of a flat-bottomed dory that is likely to be beached frequently.

Some designers and builders argue that sheathing the exterior of the hull is

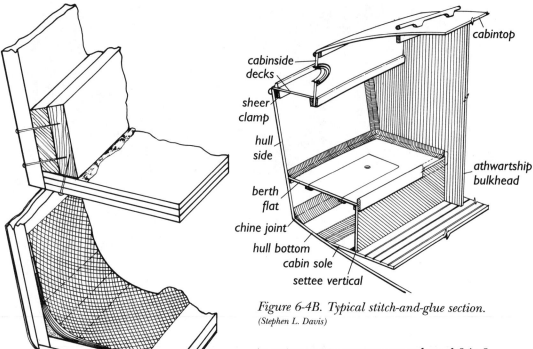

Figure 6-4B. Typical stitch-and-glue section.
(Stephen L. Davis)

Figure 6-4A. A stitch-and-glue, bottom, versus a conventional joint. (Stephen L. Davis)

unnecessary, but you should resist every temptation to skip this step because doing so will significantly decrease the longevity of your boat. I use 50-inch-wide fiberglass cloth, and at the stem, keel, and any joints where this sheathing meets, I overlap the edges to gain additional strength. Always make sure at least two layers of cloth reinforce the exterior joint seams.

For exterior sheathing of the hull and some sections of the decks, I like to use no heavier than 6-ounce woven fiberglass cloth. With anything heavier, the weave pattern will print through the final paint finish. Print-through problems seem to be on the increase lately. In our shop we go

to extremes to ensure smooth and fair finishes, but to my dismay, no matter how much care and effort we put into achieving a smooth finish, several weeks later, telltale weave patterns will appear. The darker the finish paint, the more noticeable the pattern. The epoxy companies claim that dark paint absorbs and creates too much heat and causes the epoxy to change shape slightly. The paint companies point at the epoxy as the culprit. And everybody suspects the fabric companies, who, of course, deny any problems. Frankly, I have not figured it out. The most perplexing part is that the print-through is occurring in the light colors, too, where there should not be any heat problem.

Selection of one of the harder epoxy formulations seems to reduce print-through, because the heat deformation temperature of the harder epoxy is higher than that of a more flexible system. Using

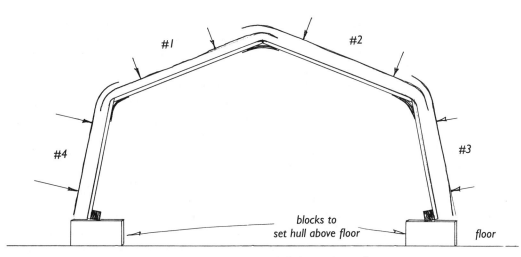

Figure 6-5. Cloth sheathing overlaps on a hull, and their sequence of application.

Figure 6-6. Topsides telegraphing—the nemesis of a dark painted hull. Is the dimpled pattern around the portlight a problem with the dark paint? Or is it a problem with the epoxy resin system? Probably it's a combination of both factors, and may be related to microscopic air bubbles entrapped in the epoxy resin and glass laminate.

4-ounce fiberglass cloth for sheathing also helps, because the finer weave of the fabric has less tendency to print-through. Finally, the longer the epoxy has cured before painting, the less noticeable the print-through.

If you insist on a dark hull color, try a simple test. Prepare two identical, fiberglass-sheathed panels matching your hull surface; paint one with your dark paint, the other with white paint. Build the panels exactly as you will build your boat, using the identical procedure for prepping and painting the surfaces. Set these freshly painted test panels in the sun, and, using an ordinary meat thermometer, check the surface temperatures. On a good hot day the dark surface may easily rise above 140°. The light-colored panel on the other hand might be just 120°F. The heat deformation temperature threshold (the point at which epoxy molecules begin to migrate and shift in relationship to each other) of most epoxies is just above that temperature. If your paint will heat the epoxy to this critical point, you may well be risking not only the fairness of the finish surface but also the integrity of the structure.

To alleviate print-through, use an epoxy system on the exterior sheathing that has the highest possible heat deformation temperature. (You might get this information from the manufacturer.) Further, consider matching it with a lightweight woven fiberglass cloth (4-ounce) to minimize the texture, and use white or a lighter color of paint to reduce the potential surface temperature of the hull and other finished surfaces. While not a panacea, these precautions will help.

For exterior sheathing you do have some choices other than fiberglass cloth, with synthetic cloths such as Xynole, Dynel, and Kevlar. In my experience, Dynel is much harder to smooth out because it stretches easier, but it will give you a very serviceable hull sheathing. My main complaint is its lack of availability. You can only buy it from one source that I know of—Defender Industries. Xynole's availability is even more limited. Kevlar is expensive, but it's a good choice where high impact resistance is required—such as the bottom of a high-speed boat used in shallow, rocky waters. My own shop skiff, a 16-foot garvey with a 40-horsepower outboard, has a Kevlar-sheathed hull. If you choose Kevlar for sheathing, be ready for a real job—much more hassle than fiberglass cloth or Dynel or Xynole. Kevlar is difficult to wet out, and unlike fiberglass cloth, it doesn't go clear when it's saturated; you can't cut it with normal scissors or razor knives and you must add a layer of fiberglass cloth before you can sand it. Vacuum bagging works well for Kevlar, but that introduces quite another set of technologies and hassles.

Some builders avoid a few of the hassles of Kevlar sheathing either by putting a layer between plies of plywood cold molding (on a big boat) or by sheathing the boat's interior. In each case it hardly seems worth the effort to gain the impact resistance that Kevlar might add—and interior sheathing makes no sense to me.

I don't know of a legitimate reason to use carbon-fiber cloth for sheathing. A plywood structure such as a stitch-and-glue boat really doesn't need carbon-fiber properties to be strong and lightweight. And carbon fiber is extremely expensive.

The bottom line is it's hard to find fault with good old readily available glass cloth for exterior sheathing. Be sure to buy one of the finishes that is epoxy-compatible. Your supplier will know which is best.

SCARFING

The overall length of the boat will determine the length of the plywood sheets you'll need. Standard marine plywood sheets measure 4 feet by 8 feet, and metric sheets (most imported plywood) measure 4 feet 1¾₆ inches by 8 feet 2⅞₆ inches. Thus, for boats longer than 7 feet 6 inches (accounting for side curvature), plywood pieces must be scarfed together with tapered, glued joints into the lengths needed.

The scarf joints between pieces need a minimum length-to-thickness ratio of 8:1, and up to 12:1 is acceptable.

The longer the glue line of the scarf, the stronger the resulting joint. A longer scarf also facilitates a more uniform bend in the scarfed section of the panel, making for a smoother hull curvature and

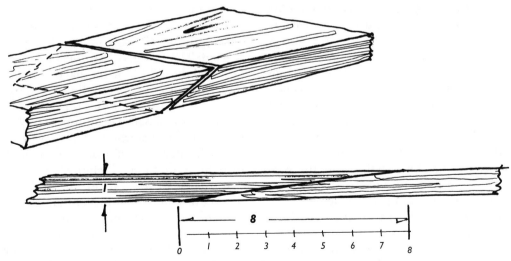

Figure 7-1. A scarf joint, top, and a side view of an 8:1 scarf ratio, bottom.

Figure 7-2. Several sheets of plywood stairstepped prior to scarfing. If the overlaps of the panels are equal, the scarfing ratio will remain consistent when the stack is planed.

shape. It's sometimes possible to purchase longer, pre-scarfed panels from specialty plywood suppliers. This is really not as expensive an option as you might think, because the freight costs will be the same whether you order 4-foot by 8-foot pieces, or longer, pre-scarfed panels. Plywood freight charges are determined by weight, not by the size of the bundle. The downside of these panels is that the quality of the scarfs may be questionable; the supplier often pays little or no attention to matching grain and color to achieve uniform panels, and occasionally even their glue-ups are mediocre, but if you're intimidated by scarfing it's a good alternative.

There are basically five methods of scarfing your own panels. The first option

is to buy a scarfing attachment that bolts to a circular saw. These attachments cut reasonably uniform bevels on the edges to be scarfed. The Gougeon Brothers market a jig called the #875 Scarffer that does amazingly well for its simplicity. It's easy to use, comes with a simple, descriptive manual, and costs about $30. The only drawback to the Scarffer is that when attached to a 7½-inch circular saw, it won't cut cleanly through more than ⅜-inch-thick plywood. You'll have to hand-plane to finish the scarf bevels on panels thicker than ⅜-inch.

The second option works quite well if you have a less-than-extensive collection of tools. Stack pieces of plywood in a staircase fashion, and with a router, hand, or power plane, knock off the "stair steps" of the stack, creating smooth and consistent bevels. Place a piece of scrap under the stack of pieces, so that it acts as the bottom stair step, cutting your bevels through to the scrap piece. I prefer this method when scarfing odd-sized panels or when I'm simply too lazy to set up my large scarfing table. Once mastered, this is also the best technique for scarfing dimensional woods to be used in masts, booms, sheer clamps, and rubrails. I consider staircase scarfing a basic method of boatbuilding, and every boatbuilder should master this technique.

The third option is to build a scarfing machine. I wouldn't recommend this for the amateur or one-time builder, but if you're building a lot of boats it might be worth the expense. I had probably built about 100 boats with the Gougeon Brothers' Scarffer when I decided that I was burning up too many circular saw motors. So, necessity being the mother of invention, I built a scarfing table on which I could cut consistent bevels using a 6-inch-wide Makita #1805B hand power planer running on rails. It is important to keep the knives on the power planer as sharp as possible. When scarfing, I keep several reserve sets of sharpened knives on hand so they can be changed quickly.

The fourth alternative for creating long panels, particularly when building a boat larger than 30 feet, is to buy your plywood in thin sheets and laminate two or three layers together with staggered butt joints. For instance, three laminations of ¼-inch or four laminations of 4mm would produce excellent planking stock for the hull of a large boat. Vacuum bagging is the best way to assure even clamping pressure while the epoxied layers cure. Laminating panels works quite well, especially for creating long panels wider than 4 feet.

The fifth method is the brainchild of John Henry, who has invented a scarfing attachment that bolts onto the base of a Makita hand power planer. A snap to use, the attachment can be adjusted to set the planer's knives at various angles.

Whether you laminate or scarf your panels, you will need a level work area with good ventilation. You can use a patio, shop floor, or even a loft, but make the surface as absolutely level as possible. If you use sawhorses to support the pieces while scarfing, be sure to level them so that the scarf joints aren't twisted or bent. Before gluing the scarfs, cover your work surface with

Figure 7-3. Using a hand power plane to straighten off the stairsteps of the plywood panels.

Figure 7-4. Final dressing with a belt sander or a grinder will finish off the scarf bevels. Note the consistent lines of veneer layers in the plywood panels. When dressed these lines will be perfectly straight and even.

plastic to prevent excess epoxy from fouling it. Have your work area and materials fully prepared before you start, because once the bevels are coated with epoxy, there is no time to waste as you position and clamp the panels. I coat the beveled edges with unthickened epoxy a full 15 to 20 minutes before assembling the scarf joints. Doing so allows the epoxy to soak into the end grain, avoiding the possibility of a weakened, epoxy-starved joint. Just before final assembly, I recoat the mating edges with epoxy thickened slightly with wood flour or Cabosil.

The simplest method I have found for applying pressure while clamping and glu-ing multiple pieces is to use weights or props from an overhead beam. Any kind of weights will work. I have found that placing the weights on stiff 2-inch x 6-inch or 2-inch x 8-inch boards spreads the pressure more uniformly on the stack of panels.

I use light nails or staples to pin the panels in position until clamp pressure can be applied. Be sure to place plastic between the panel layers if you are scarfing several panels at a time to prevent excess epoxy from laminating them together. For good clamp pressure when you're just clamping a few pieces, use long drywall screws and a drill motor to screw a stiff piece of wood over the top of the panels

Figure 7-5. Weights stacked on pinned and glued scarfs can provide enough pressure to ensure a good scarf lamination. If you're gluing the scarfs, be sure to put plastic between plywood layers so excess epoxy will not seep out and glue your panels together.

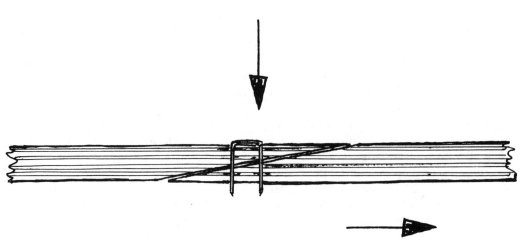

*Figure 7-6. A nail or staple through a scarf prevents slippage caused by
the downward pressure of clamps or weights.*

into a wood base or piece of stock on the bottom of the stack. Make certain the drywall screws reach all the way through the pile. I space the screws about 6 to 10 inches apart in staggered rows. They have to be withdrawn after the scarfs are glued and cured, and an epoxy-and-wood-flour paste used to patch the holes.

Be sure that the mating surfaces of the scarf are flat and smooth by moving a small stick of wood back and forth across the glue line to check the scarf's alignment. Allow a couple of days for the epoxy to cure fully, then sand the excess glue from the scarf joints.

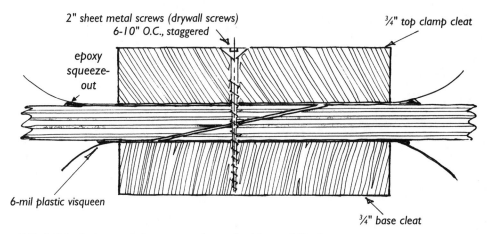

*Figure 7-7. A 2-inch sheet metal screw can be used with wood blocks to
clamp a joint.*

8

LOFTING

For a stitch-and-glue boat, lofting simply means taking the designed panel shapes and drawing them, full-size, on sheets of marine plywood. As in traditional boat-building, the lofting process is the most important stage of building. The final shape of the boat is dictated by the panel shapes; at stake are a pleasing appearance, efficient hydrodynamics, and overall performance. Any unfairness in the underwater panels will quickly affect the coefficient of drag and change the way the boat moves through the water. If the lines of the hull are in any way crooked, uneven, or unfair, the result will be ungainly appearance and a boat out of proportion. While it would be possible for a designer to provide full-sized patterns for a stitch-and-glue boat, and save you a lofting step, paper patterns are unstable, and the results could be inaccurate and unpredictable. The lofting process requires such a small amount of time that little is to be gained from providing full-sized patterns.

Think of a stitch-and-glue boat as if it were a banana. If you were to peel a banana, eat the fruit, and then reassemble the peels, you would have a banana shape again. Furthermore, if you traced the shape of each flattened segment of peel onto cardboard or kraft paper, you could then cut out and assemble a paper model of the banana. In essence that is exactly what a boat designer does with a stitch-and-glue design. He or she imagines the boat's shape as a collection of large peels, or component parts, with their edges lying on the sheer, chine and, keel lines of the boat. In lofting the stitch-and-glue boat, all you are doing is taking the designer's outlines for the peels (panels) and drawing them full-size on flat plywood sheets. If you choose to build a boat design that was not originally drawn for stitch-and-glue construction, it becomes a little more complicated. You'll have to follow the process described in Chapter 9 to generate your own peels or panel dimensions.

Drawing the full-sized panels is a simple procedure. For the simplest shape, a V-bottomed hull, there are only two side panels, two bottom panels, and a transom. With larger designs, the lofting requires drawing full-sized bulkheads and additional interior members to strengthen the hull athwartships (side-to-side) and longitudinally (fore-and-aft). Any one of these many panels or

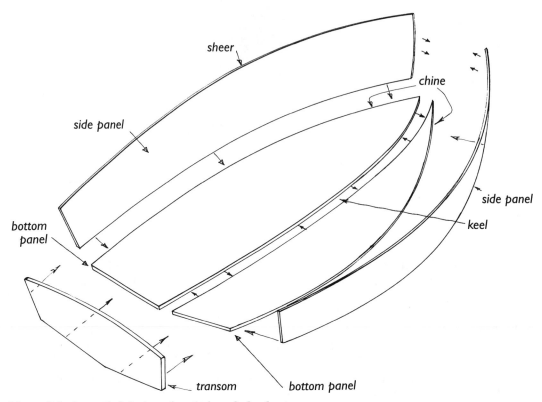

Figure 8-1. An exploded view of a stitch-and-glue boat.

interior parts can drastically affect the final symmetry and aesthetics of the hull, so each panel or part must be lofted and proofed as accurately as possible. We will go into proofing in Chapter 13.

When lofting, if the boats are small enough to make this practical, I prefer to lay the marine plywood on sawhorses to avoid working on my knees. This might not be practical with bigger boats; lay the plywood on some wooden cleats on the floor and you can cut without your saw blade hitting the floor. Whichever method you prefer, the panels must be level and flat. If the floor is uneven, begin by laying out and leveling battens (sticks) every 12 to 18 inches. Accuracy in lofting depends par-

tially on how level the panels are while you mark the station and dimension points. Usually, station marks are at 12-inch intervals along the plywood's long edges. It really makes no difference what intervals the designer has indicated, however, as long as you are faithful when determining and setting the true dimension marks.

When setting station marks, I use a drywall T-square with a 50-inch leg to mark the full width of the panel; this speeds up the process. If you have only a carpenter's framing or L-square, simply extend one leg by attaching a batten. Be sure to double-check all station marks for accuracy.

Once the station marks are satisfactory, begin to project the dimension marks

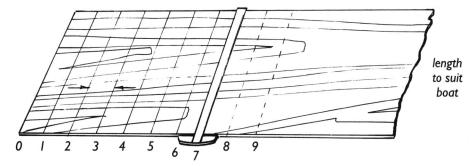

Figure 8-2. Mark off stations with a drywall square.

onto the panels. The rule to remember is *feet-inches-eighths*—the universal three-numeral designation for boatbuilders locating exact dimension points by measuring distances along given station marks. Hence, 3–4–2 on a blueprint translates to 3 feet, 4 inches, 2⁄8 inches from the edge of the plywood panel. The third numeral is eighths, never fourths, or halves, or anything else. The only possible variable might be a plus (+) or minus (–) sign; if these should appear, it translates to plus or minus a sixteenth of an inch. Thus, 2–5–5+ translates to 2 feet 5¹¹⁄₁₆ inches. The

more you use these triple numerals, the more second nature it will become.

With all the dimension points in place, the next step is to place a batten along the points to draw the curved lines (the edges of our banana peels). Do this by driving small nails on each side of the batten along its length so that the batten aligns to all the dimension marks. Be sure to avoid the temptation of nailing through the batten. Not only would that ruin a perfectly good batten, but it immediately affects the true curvature of the line by not allowing you to adjust for fairness along the length of the

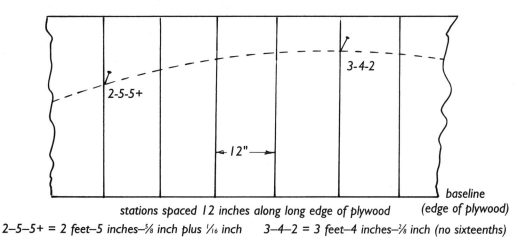

stations spaced 12 inches along long edge of plywood

baseline (edge of plywood)

2–5–5+ = 2 feet–5 inches–⅝ inch plus ¹⁄₁₆ inch   3–4–2 = 3 feet–4 inches–²⁄₈ inch (no sixteenths)

Figure 8-3. Station marks and lofting on plywood.

batten. Good battens of clear, vertical-grain wood with uniform flexibility are hard to find, so think of your batten as a tool. You would never dream of nailing through the wooden handles of other tools; *do not nail through your batten.*

When lofting, you want the curves to be as smooth as possible, without bumps or hollows, and you'll need a batten that will flex uniformly throughout its length. The smoothness of a batten's curvature will be affected if one section is either more stiff or more flexible than the rest of the batten. Step back after aligning the batten, and move from side to side, sighting the curvature along the batten's whole length. Take note of any flat areas in the curvature, and look for bumps that might be caused by improper positioning of a nail or by the earlier mismarking of a dimension point. If the curve is a severe one, you may need to set additional nail guides to achieve a fair line; then again, if the curve

is soft, you'll need fewer nail guides to allow the batten to flex smoothly.

In the end, the batten has to find its proper level of tension. The bow section of the plywood panels, where the curves are more pronounced, are the most difficult and critical; here you must be absolutely faithful to the designer's dimensions and not attempt to average or straighten out lines.

When you are satisfied that the dimension marks are correct and the batten is flexing smoothly over its full length, connect all the dimension marks. Keep the pencil at a constant angle to the batten over the full length of the curve. Use your free hand to hold the batten down to avoid shifting or pushing it with the pencil. Repeat the procedure and mark all the edges of the panels.

You have now drawn in large scale the outlines of the boat's panels. Next you'll cut them out.

Figure 8-4. A batten held in position with small nails. Note that the loftsman presses down the batten to prevent it from shifting as he marks the lines of the faired panel.

9

MODELING

Though it may seem like a trivial pursuit at first, the modeling process is essential to consolidating ideas about form, symmetry, and the details of the final design. It is helpful to make a model of a design before building the boat, as the steps are similar. In modeling, the builder gains understanding and confidence about the steps of construction, ideas about the look and feel of the boat, solid notions about color schemes, and details for all manner of modifications. The modeling process can also be used to establish a design's hydrostatics and power requirements, thus giving the designer or builder clues to the full-size weight, center of buoyancy, and likely speed of the design.

A stitch-and-glue project is so radically different from almost any other boatbuilding method that going through the steps on a model can open a builder's eyes and help him or her visualize the full-scale project.

What if the boat you really want to build isn't available through the usual design sources? Well, you can commission a custom design, of course, but your budget may not permit that. A less expensive alternative is to adapt one of the many existing plywood-on-frame designs for stitch-and-glue construction. Plywood-on-frame designs proliferated for decades going back to World War II and earlier, and a rich stock of them exists. Most can be adapted with some time and effort to draw up the panel plans and make the structural conversions.

A few years ago I found myself in a telephone discussion with John Ratzenberger. John, who starred as Cliff Claven on the television program *Cheers*, was interested in a new catboat. After several weeks, we settled on Ted Brewer's 22-foot Cape Cod catboat. It was designed, however, for traditional sheet-plywood construction rather than stitch-and-glue construction. Given John's limited schedule, shuttling between Hollywood and his home in the Northwest, I felt that a conversion of the Cape Cod design from plywood-on-frame to stitch-and-glue construction would be appropriate. The stitch-and-glue boat could be built faster and easier, and from John's point of view, it would provide simpler maintenance and better service over the long run. But could it be done? And how much work would

Figure 9-1. John Ratzenberger and his Ted Brewer–designed catboat modified for stitch-and-glue construction.

the stitch-and-glue conversion entail?

At that time, in fourteen years of designing and building boats, I had never built to another designer's plan. It wasn't that the option didn't exist, but simply that I enjoy designing a boat and then seeing the project through to launching. But this case was an exception. I wanted to build the catboat for John, and I liked the Brewer design, so why reinvent the wheel? After a phone call to Ted Brewer to get his thoughts on converting the design to stitch-and-glue construction, and after arriving at an agreed price for the boat with Mr. Ratzenberger, the project was a go.

The original design called for complicated, heavy framing that would have been extremely difficult to seal with epoxy. It also required many mechanical fasteners that would have obstructed and jeopardized the protective epoxy coating. A complicated backbone or building setup is required before the boatbuilding could commence, and finally, the many parts in the framing demanded careful layout and lofting to achieve a fair hull. The more parts there were, the greater the chances of compromising a hull's fairness and maintainability.

With the endorsement of the designer, who was enthusiastic about having the plans revised to appeal to a wider audience, I set myself on the path of converting the plywood-on-frame design to a stitch-and-glue design.

Over the years, I have found that the

Figure 9-2. No boxy shapes: Czarinna's fantail stern.

most difficult information to obtain for a new or modified design is the correct shape of the hull panels. Precise design of these panels is my greatest concern, since any compromise there may distort the hull shape from its designed specifications. Indeed, any flaws in the panel shapes can be magnified in the final hull shape.

In my own, still-evolving path of designing, I have used four different methods to generate the shapes and dimensions of stitch-and-glue panels. The only real limitation is the degree to which a sheet of plywood can bend or conform to the shape required. I have always been concerned about achieving a boat that will function well while presenting an aesthetically pleasing appearance. The traditionalist in me always wants to avoid the stereotypical

plywood box shape at all costs. Just because one uses plywood sheets to construct a boat does not mean that the results have to look flat and constrained.

INTUITIVE DESIGN

Early in my career I used an intuitive approach to finding the shapes of panels. This method depends heavily on previous experience with plywood shapes. I would begin by cutting out small-scale hull panels from thin sheets of balsa, and in a few evenings, several hull shapes could be generated by regulating the outline shapes of the panels and the depths of the dart cuts in the bottoms. This kind of exercise went a long way toward acquainting me with the many potential combinations of panel shapes and their folded results, and the finite limits of plywood bending. The problem was that the shapes of the panels were generated *before* the lines of the finished hull. It was difficult to draw an accurate representation of the model's lines after it was assembled, even though the panel shapes were accurate. Dimensions that should come from the drawings had to be taken later from the full-sized boat, after cutting and fitting the hull's many pieces. Only after several boats were built to the same panel dimensions would I arrive at reasonably accurate dimensions of the finished hull.

Nevertheless, through intuitive modeling, I designed several boats up to 30 feet long which, even today, I find interesting and at times more complex than many of my later designs. This method led me to the 20-foot scow sloop Lichen a couple of years ago. The shape of that design was unconventional enough to defy proper sketching, yet somehow I knew the result I wanted. I started that project by cutting out shapes of thin (1/32-inch) aircraft plywood, and quickly came up with the hull I was looking to build.

What I had been unable to sketch I was able to model. I like to think that how you get there is never as important as the final expression. Maybe it was a classic right brain–left brain dilemma.

CARVED HALF-MODELS

The second way to get the panel shapes of a stitch-and-glue design is to carve a chined, solid half-model to small scale (3/4" or 1" = 1'), then cover the model with tracing paper and trace the hull's panel outlines on the paper. When these tracings are laid out flat and the outlines faired with a drafting batten, you get reasonably accurate and acceptable small-scale panel shapes.

Using solid half-models always appealed to my sense of tradition; it is, after all, close to the tried, true, and traditional approach to design. But what comes first, the model or the hull lines drawings? Realistically, the answer is a complicated combination of both, and the end result is usually a manifestation of some vague vision of what looks most pleasing to the designer. I always began by sketching a set of preliminary lines in an attempt to define the rough edges or parameters of the design. When satisfied with those lines, I moved to the workbench and carved the half-model. (The negative side of the half-model approach is the difficulty of accurately representing all the parts of the full-sized boat.)

In most cases, while making the half-model I would revise the initial shape of the hull to improve its appearance. Then I would go back to the drawing board and redraw the lines of the boat to match the half-model. The danger is that every step from the drawing board to the half-model and back again compounds the chances for error. The resulting design was sometimes so far afield from its original intent that I abandoned (or should have abandoned) the whole project. But the biggest drawback is the time invested in drawing, modeling, and redrawing, which tended to sap my inspiration level for the boat.

I needed a quicker and more open-ended method of designing, with less chance for error. And in the case of the Cape Cod catboat conversion project for John, I needed to stay true to the original Brewer-designed lines. From past experience with the half-model method,

I knew its accuracy would be questionable and that any changes would be tantamount to producing a newer version of the design. I was determined not to walk that path, both in respect for Ted Brewer's original lines and because if I had wanted to do a full custom design badly enough, I would have proposed that right from the start.

COMPUTER-ASSISTED DESIGN (CAD) SYSTEMS

The third method for generating panel dimensions is with computer-assisted design, or CAD. To my eye, CAD lines on a screen can't compare with a tactile, three-dimensional half-hull model. The computer software presently available may be state of the art, but it leaves a lot to be desired in the accuracy of the information it generates and its ease of use. When generating the panel information (plate projections, in software language), the computer takes a complicated mathematical look at the hull with a specific series of calculations. But the math base may not like some part of the boat's form—a problem I've encountered in two different CAD programs in the past few years. The Czarinna series and the Oysta 42 have rounded fantail sterns, and the CAD programs could not project the sterns properly. The only way to get around the mathematical limitations of the software was to break the boats into bow and stern segments, then splice them together with the computer. The splice had to be extremely accurate and there was almost no way to fair between the two halves. The effort involved much trial and error, and made for some frustrating moments.

Further, most of the computer programs will make the lines conform to developed conical surfaces, while not telling the designer how—or where—to alter the original design's lines. This automatic process creates a problem if one wants to learn intuitively about hull shapes. Every set of computer-generated hull panels I have built from has presented some small, but irritating, error that required correction and compensation. And without a fair bit of experience under my belt I might not have spotted the error, and ended up with a real disaster.

Of course, I'm referring to the low-cost CAD packages, not the six- and seven-figure ship-design software programs. Most boatbuilders do not have ready access to the necessary hardware and software; even the simplest comprehensive CAD software costs well into five figures. One alternative is to locate a designer who regularly uses CAD and subcontract the panel conversion work. In fact, I decided to do just that, and through Ted Brewer's lead, I found Jack Beaton from Coast Yacht Design in Vancouver, British Columbia, who generated all the panel information for us. But as it turned out, I could not obtain Beaton's computer-generated information fast enough to meet John Ratzenberger's contracted construction schedule. Pressed by a tight timetable, I put on my thinking cap and came up with a fourth method.

PANELED HALF-MODELS

What I came up with I call the paneled half-model, and it's the simplest, quickest, and most accurate method I've used. It produces a three-dimensional model that can be quickly understood by someone without special skills. The builder can take the lines off any existing chined design, and by building a paneled half-model translate the design into stitch-and-glue panel shapes. If needed, the mirror image can be constructed so that scale model testing can be done for flotational characteristics such as loading, displacement, and appearance.

My approach was to reduce the boat to the fewest, simplest lines necessary to describe it. Then I translate those lines into the fewest number of parts that will comprise its three-dimensional shape. The side view, or profile, of a simple V-bottomed boat would show the sheer of the boat as line #1, the chine as line #2, the fairbody line as line #3, and the transom either as line #4 or the continuation of the other lines, in the case of a fantail stern or a double-ender. Remember that the fewer the lines used to represent the design, the greater the potential accuracy.

The profile of the boat contains only half the information necessary for an accurate scale model, though. The other half is provided by the half-breadth, or top, view, which is the view a sea gull enjoys just before he fertilizes your deck. This view gives the deck outline and the width of the transom at the sheer; the chine outline; and the half-beams from the fore-and-aft centerline to the sheer or chine at an infinite number of stations or points. Note also the perpendicular line from the outside corner of the transom and chine to the centerline.

To build an accurate planked half model, four shapes are required: (1) the longitudinal profile of the boat without any keel or appendages, showing the chine position; (2) the outline of the half-deck (sheer plane) viewed from the top; (3) the outline of the half-chine plane viewed from the top; and (4) the shape of the

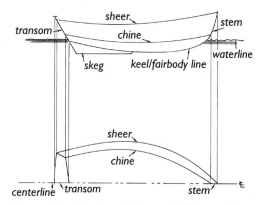

Figure 9-3. The simple lines of a V-bottomed boat in profile and half-breadth views.

transom. Think of these four basic shapes as the skeleton over which the skin is drawn. If your design is multichined, you will need the extra chine planes and their positions marked on the profile.

Using an enlarging photocopier, you can enlarge the plans to the desired half-model scale, but be aware that photocopier enlarging is never perfectly accurate. Whether you are using lines taken off a boat or the actual blueprints of a design, if you want extremely accurate lines, go to

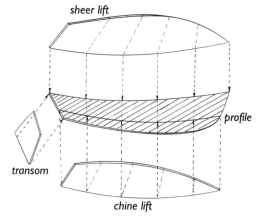

Figure 9-4. The four basic shapes of a boat.

a printer and have a camera enlargement made. Or you can take the table of offsets and loft a scaled view of the boat yourself to the larger scale.

I recommend working to the largest scale practical, and one that can be conveniently read with an architect's scale rule. At least, try to end up with a model between 20 and 30 inches long. The scale you use may range from ¾ inch to 3 inches to the foot. The larger the model the potentially more accurate your half-model and your panel projections will be.

I prefer to use ¼-inch plywood for the model's profile and ⅛-inch plywood (doorskins) for the sheer and chine lifts. You can also use dimensional solid wood planed to the ¼- or ⅛-inch thicknesses. The easiest way to transfer the lines of the boat to your modeling stock is using a pounce wheel (toothed wheel) or pinpricks through the paper onto the stock so that you won't ruin the original drawings. If you use pinpricks, fair the lines between the marks with a small batten. If you prefer, you can use carbon paper to transfer the drawing onto tracing paper. Then glue the tracing paper to the stock directly and cut out the parts.

Unless the boat has a perfectly flat sheer or chine (parallel to the waterline in profile), the top view of the boat plan is not showing you the actual, unbent or expanded shape of the sheer and chine planes. For an accurate half model, you'll need to do a simple conversion drawing to obtain the true shape. Starting with the sheer, bend a light batten along the sheerline on the profile from the side view. Assuming you began with the plans for a plywood-on-frame boat, the chances are good that the original drawing will include some station lines, so make a small mark on the batten where each of the station marks intersects the sheer. If your plan

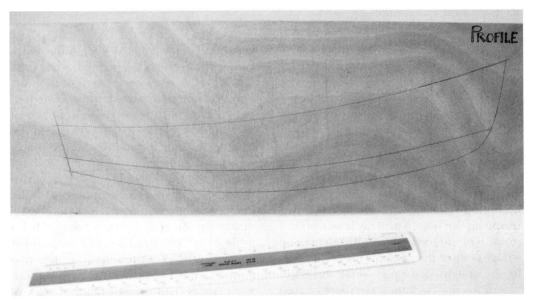

Figure 9-5. The catboat's profile is shown on the plywood that will be used for making the model.

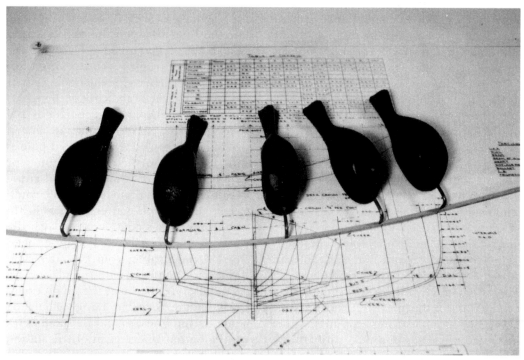

Figure 9-6. Spring a batten to the curve of the sheer in profile, and mark its intersections with the stations.

does not show station marks, you will need to choose and place your own stations for reference. The station marks need to be shown on both the profile and the top view of the design, aligning accurately between the two views. I use a minimum of ten stations on the two views to give an accurate reading of offsets.

Once the bent batten is marked at each station on the profile drawing, including the bow and stern ends, unspring the batten and lay it out on the stock to be cut for the sheer lift. Using one straight side of the stock for the centerline, lay the straightened batten along this edge. *(If you run the grain of the ⅛-inch plywood perpendicular to the centerline, the plywood will bend to the sheer rocker with greater ease and*

accuracy.) Mark each of the station mark intersections along the previously bent batten, as well as the intersections of the stem and transom points, then draw a line perpendicular to the centerline on each of these marks. Now you can go back to the original drawing to pick off the next pieces of needed information.

On the top-view plan, using a pair of dividers or a paper tick-strip, measure the half-beams of each station from the centerline to the sheerline. (If your design has a table of offsets, use this information for half-breadths.) Transfer this information to the stock for the sheer lift at each station, then connect those half-beam marks on the station lines with a flexible batten to draw the new outline of the unbent deck

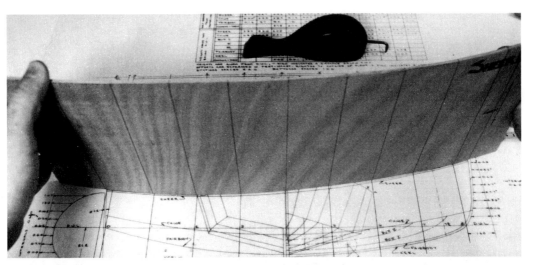

Figure 9-7. The plywood panel that will become the sheer lift is shown sprung into place over the drawing.

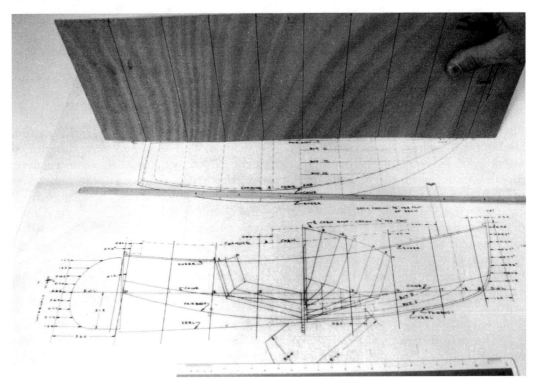

Figure 9-8. Note how the projected spacings change when the plywood is straightened.

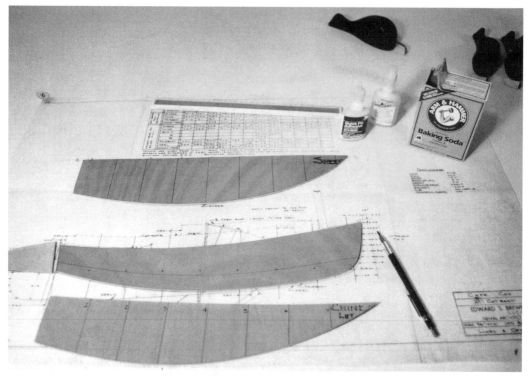

Figure 9-9. The sheer lift, the chine lift, profile, and transom will form the skeleton of the half model.

lift. Unless the boat has a straight sheer parallel to the waterline, the true, stretched-out sheer lift will be slightly longer than the top view indicated in the design. Repeat this process for the chine lift.

Once the sheer and chine lifts are drawn, the sheer lift can be overlapped on top of the profile cutout and the thickness of the lift cut away from the top of the profile. The chine lift will need the thickness of the profile cutout deducted from its width so that it will reflect the true designed half-beam.

I have found that a paneled half-model is best built from hull dimensions measured to the inside of the planking, since the full-sized stitch-and-glue shell is thin enough that the hydrodynamics will not change significantly. If, however, you make a half-model of an older design not conceived for stitch-and-glue construction, check whether the designer intended for the lines to be on the inside or outside of the planking. By building to the inside of the hull design, your interior framework and lifts do not need to have the thickness of the hull plating subtracted from the edges of the hull lifts, which would be arduous to do accurately.

Use a cyanoacrylate (CA) glue for bonding the parts of the half-model. Most hobby shops carry cyanoacrylates, an advanced cousin of the instant glues found in your local hardware and drug stores. I like a brand called Zap-a-Gap, which works well with wood and the exacting fits necessary for the half-model. I also use an accelerator with the Zap-a-Gap, called Zip Kicker. Used in combination, these products will set up instantly, helping to assure perfect alignment. If you tend to work on the sloppy side, purchase Z-7 Debonder to help unglue mistakes. I read recently that accelerators for the cyanoacrylates may be damaging to the ozone layer, so a perfectly good option is to use baking soda. It is not as fast an accelerator as Zip Kicker, but it is kinder to the Earth. I apply glue to the parts to be bonded then sprinkle a pinch of soda onto the wet glue. A few seconds later the bond is set.

Another helpful tool for fitting and beveling parts is a simple rasp made up of a ¾-inch x 1-inch x 6-inch block of wood wrapped in a piece of 80-grit sandpaper.

Once you have cut out all the parts for the profile, deck lift, chine lift, and transom, and you have marked the position of the chine line on the profile, you can begin the assembly of the half-model. I use tabs of glue about ½ inch apart to glue the lifts to the profile. Apply three or four tabs, add the accelerator, and allow it to set up before moving to the next section. Use reinforced filament strapping (packaging)

Figure 9-11. A wood block wrapped with sandpaper makes a simple rasp for beveling the lifts.

tape to help hold the panels together while gluing. When you glue the chine lift to the profile, be sure to place the lift just above the line that defines the chine position.

As you place the two lifts on the profile, they must be exactly perpendicular to the profile. Plywood tends to bend well on only one axis, so the lifts will hold their true position better if the grain in the chine and sheer lifts is perpendicular to the profile. (If your design has a strong sheer, you should consider using Italian poplar plywood—or bender board—as it will bend truer to the sheer.) The profile must be perfectly flat—it's usually easiest to attach it to a thick, flat platen (slab of scrap wood) with a dab or two of glue. The centerline of the two lifts must contact the profile at all points. If you have persistent problems holding the lifts perpendicular while gluing, cut out small, 90-degree squares from the door skin and glue them

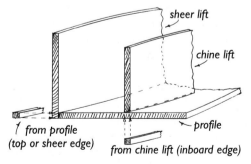

Figure 9-10. Deduct the thickness of the sheer lift and profile to compensate for the thickness of the stock.

in place to maintain the perpendicular positions of the lifts.

The next step is to attach the transom to the profile and the chine lift. After the parts are glued together, you are ready to glue the skin over the half-model to achieve the boat's finished shape. You'll need to bevel the keel, stem, and deck edges of the profile and the sheer lift to accurately attach the hull skin to the half-model later, properly compensating for the planking angle. Run the sandpaper back and forth on the edges. Complete the beveling of the keel and stern first, and panel the half-model's bottom before going on to bevel the deck edge of the sheer lift.

I like to use modeler's ⅟₃₂-inch, three-ply birch aircraft plywood for planking the half-model, because this type of plywood bends exactly in the scale model as the full-sized plywood does in the full-sized boat. An alternative is the ⅟₃₂-inch Formica-type laminate used by cabinetmakers in the European-style cabinets so popular in contemporary house construction. This laminate is half the thickness of the standard ⅟₁₆-inch countertop grades, and it's readily available, economical, and best of all, pre-colored—which means you can avoid painting your half-model later. It cuts cleanly and precisely with good quality scissors, and glues well.

To panel the bottom, cut the plywood or laminate somewhat larger than the panel needed, and put a few drops of glue on the forwardmost section of both the profile and the chine lift. Glue from bow to stern, holding the panel in position with package strapping tape while the glue sets. With the bottom panel glued in place and trimmed to shape with a single-edge razor blade or an X-Acto knife, you can now bevel the sheer lift. Again, work with the sandpaper rasp until the edge of the lift is properly beveled to receive the side panel. Use the rasp with the sandpaper only on the upper portion of the block where it will contact just the sheer lift. In that fashion, you will bevel the sheer lift and not affect the bottom paneling or chine lift.

You can now cut out a side panel and glue it onto the lifts, working from bow to stern. Once the glue has set, do the final trimming of the edges of the panels on the hull.

If you intend to attach the cabin structures to the hull, this is the time to panel those parts. The layout of all cabin structures is much easier if they are included in the profile of the half-model at the beginning. Attaching separate pieces is more difficult if each alignment has to be done separately.

The easiest way to finish the model is to prime the entire boat with a sandable primer, available at the hardware store. Put two coats of primer on your model, then sand using 80-grit sandpaper for the rough spots and 150-grit for the rest of the hull after the first application. When the second coat of primer has dried, fill

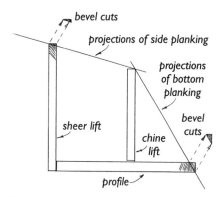

Figure 9-12. Beveling is essential before attaching the hull skin.

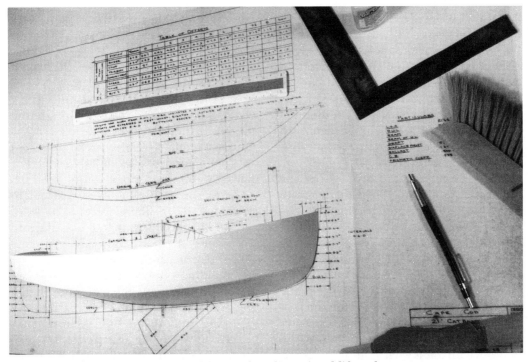

Figure 9-13. The completed hull model gives three-dimensional life to the two-dimensional drawings.

any remaining bad spots and use 220-grit sandpaper to sand the entire hull smooth and fair.

For the finish coat, use a fast-drying spray enamel. The results are very smooth, and you'll save time when applying thin multiple coats, with 15 to 20 minutes between coats.

Take great care in masking the other structures before you paint. Accent colors can be used for the deck and cabin areas. And, when the painting is done, you can use automotive pin striping to show the waterline, the deck rails, and window edges. A contrasting color below the boot stripe will realistically accent the model. If it's done carefully, a planked half-model can become a real mantelpiece.

TRANSFERRING PANEL INFORMATION

When the half-model is built accurately, and the hull is fair and true without any twist or irregularity, you can extract the true expanded shapes of the hull panels. I have found that Mylar, a plastic drafting film available from office supply stores, is the easiest material to use for picking off the panel projections. Mylar is translucent, and if you use a couple of drops of cyanoacrylate glue to lightly tack it in place on the model, you can trace extremely accurate outlines of the panel shapes, then easily remove it. Tracing paper will work, but you can't glue it to the model without its tearing when removed.

Make a series of small pencil dots along the panel edges, taking care while marking the chine and sheer panels that the Mylar does not pucker or fold anywhere. It must be flat against each surface with full contact for the entire length of the panel. This also will be the final check on whether the design can be fully developed from plywood, because Mylar, like plywood, only bends well in one dimension.

After removing the Mylar from the half-model and fairing the panel lines with a flexible batten through the pencil dots, you are ready to do the conversions for the full-scale panels. Measure the lofting points on 12-inch scaled stations (e.g., if your model is scaled 1 inch to the foot, take measurements off the Mylar at stations 1 inch apart). Use the "feet-inches-eighths" dimensional indications. After you've transferred the panel shapes, the only decision left is what scantlings—thickness of plywood and other structures—to use in the full-scale boat (see Chapter 10).

BUILDING A FULL FLOTATION MODEL

If you plan to tank-test your model, use the ¾" = 1' scale. At this scale, the model's towing speed will be exactly 25 percent of the full-size boat's potential speed. When I tow a test model, I weight the model down to the designed waterline. Pulling it behind a skiff at, say, 4 mph, I use a video camera to record the model's response, thereby approximating the design's full-size performance at 16 mph. Later, watching the video and freezing frames, I can analyze the bow wave and the wake action; sometimes even the effectiveness of the spray rail or trim tabs can be noted. (See Weston Farmer's *From My Old Boat Shop*,

International Marine, 1979, Chapters 12 and 13. This book is out of print but available from libraries.)

In the ¾-inch-scale model, the weight of the model is related to the full-size boat by the cube of the linear ratio. Use a vegetable or meat scale to weigh the model. If the linear scale ratio is 16:1, a 1-pound model's weight can be projected to 4,096 pounds for the full-size boat. For ballast weight, a copper penny in ¾-inch scale translates to a roughly full-size weight of 25 pounds. It can be great fun to check out the weights of engines, fuel tanks, and everything else that might affect the centers of balance and gravity in the boat.

Building a flotation model is most easily done by following the half-model building procedure and simply gluing lifts and planking up both sides of the boat's profile. If you've already procured your panel-shape information from a half-model or you've purchased a design made for stitch-and-glue construction, you can build your flotation model in scale as you would a full-scale version—simply cutting out the panels of the boat and using nylon-filament packing tape (available from any drug or postal store) instead of wires to stitch the boat. 5 Minute epoxy or CA glue can be used in lieu of epoxy and glass joints as in the full-sized boat.

Loft and cut out the bottom panels as outlined in Chapter 8 and lay one atop the other in a mirror image. Fasten the panels along the keel line with 1½-inch-long strips of strapping tape, then spread them out to form the bottom shape. If you have trouble holding the panels apart, cut a small stick to use as a bottom spreader. Tape the side panels to the bottom panels, and place small scrapwood sticks as sheer spreaders to spread the top of the model open. Assuming you have a stitch-and-glue design, you can go further with your scale boatbuilding and build the whole structure complete with bulkheads and all. Glue together the keel lines and chine lines with 5 Minute epoxy or CA glue, and then cut out and install the bulkheads. Assemble the rest of the boat by cutting each component until it fits properly, gluing it only when you're sure it is properly shaped and positioned. Wherever you find a need for adjustment, make these changes in colored ink on your blueprints; these notations may become very important information later. This is probably the greatest benefit of the whole modeling exercise—it gives you a scale glimpse into the building process.

Once you have the primary structure fitted and glued into place, turn to the keel, stem, and deck structures. Literally every part of the actual boat should go on the scale model to generate the most possible information from visualization and tow testing. There is an obvious limit to the detailing, but the true modeling enthusiast will want to work in every last detail possible, including testing out paint colors and schemes.

After painting, or at least sealing, the finished model is ready for tow testing. Or, you may simply want to place it on your mantelpiece or keep it near your workbench. I have many times found a model helpful in keeping me inspired and motivated while working on the full-sized version.

10

SCANTLINGS

Because it's capable of building boats from small dinghies up to 80-footers, the stitch-and-glue medium obviously has a large amount of versatility. A stitch-and-glue boat larger than a dinghy or skiff will be subject to considerably more stress than the smaller boat, and it will need additional structure to tie together the strong exterior shell of the vessel and help keep it rigid.

Two basic types of structure help with these loads: stringers and bulkheads.

Stringers are longitudinal beams, usually laminated in place, running from bow to stern in as uninterrupted a manner as possible. Gunwales in small boats and sheer clamps in large boats fall into the stringer category. Stringers usually are made from dimensional stock, though there are exceptions where parts, or indeed the entire stringer, might be laminated from plywood. My Surf Scoter, a raised-deck design, has so much shape in a portion of its sheer clamp that it precludes using dimensional stock. It would simply be too weak. Laminating it from several layers of plywood cut to shape, though, is strong and works well.

Figure 10-1. Sawn-to-shape plywood sheer clamp lamination in the cockpit of the 22-foot Surf Scoter. Note the notch cutout in the bulkhead to let in the sheer clamp. The lower intermediate sheer clamp has already been laminated into place, and due to its straighter run, doesn't need to be sawn to shape.

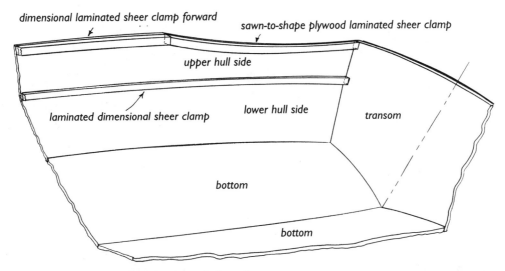

Figure 10-2. A sawn-to-shape laminated sheer clamp.

Stringers are always glued in place, then reinforced with mechanical fasteners. In many instances I've used stringers to land other structures, which effectively helps spread loads.

Bulkheads, the other basic structure in a stitch-and-glue boat, are cut from large marine plywood sheets and are set either athwartships, longitudinally, or flat. Think of the stitch-and-glue boat as an old-fashioned egg crate, with an outside box, and partitions erected at 90-degree angles to each other to hold the eggs and prevent the crate from being crushed. The stitch-and-glue boat works in much the same manner, distributing stress and loads through a gridwork of bulkheads while protecting cargo and occupants in the various compartments. Stresses must be distributed throughout the structure so no single area carries a disproportionate strain.

Bulkheads provide a definition of space as well as support. A galley compartment, for example, can be created using structural bulkheads. It makes sense to use

the bulkhead system to create needed space and increase the hull's overall strength. By bonding each piece of ply-

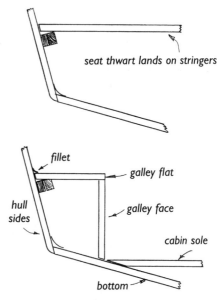

Figure 10-3. Two structural stringers with attaching parts.

71

Figure 10-4. The 29-foot Means of Grace design showing a perspective of the bulkheads and framing structure of a large stitch-and-glue boat.

wood and every stick of dimensional wood with epoxy and fiberglass composite joints, every component becomes structural.

Bulkheads can double as berth faces, berth flats, cabin soles, cockpit soles, cabin sides, decks, cabintops, galley faces, galley flats, head bulkheads, engine beds, anchor locker bulkheads, and more.

As for the thicknesses of these bulkheads, when I first began building boats, I used fir plywood in the hulls. But not being fond of fir's appearance, I always painted it. I wanted the option of varnishing some interior parts, so I began using ½-inch mahogany plywood simply because the local supply was good. When my source disappeared, however, I tried ¾-inch

mahogany bulkheads and was surprised to find such a significant improvement in rigidity. During the building of the boat, the ½-inch bulkheads were comparatively hard to keep straight and square. The ¾-inch plywood was far more rigid and fit true—and its additional weight was more than compensated by its stiffness and ease of use.

Certainly, if I were constructing a multihull or racing monohull, overall weight would be a concern. If keeping weight to a minimum is important, you might use bulkheads made from one of the balsa-foam-, or honeycomb-core materials. These are considerably lighter than solid plywood, but they cost much more per panel. For normal cruising and inter-mediate-performance designs, I use ¾-inch marine plywood for all major athwartships and longitudinal bulkheads and for any flat surface that can be jumped or walked on or subjected to severe strain. For a component well supported by a primary framing structure, I use ½-inch plywood.

When selecting stitch-and-glue skin thickness, always think stiffer, sturdier, and stronger, and consider the service duty of the boat. For instance, in my Surf Scoter design, the displacement scantlings would indicate a skin of 12mm, or ½ inch. But the majority of the Surf Scoters will be either dry-sailed from a trailer or will live on a

trailer while wintering. That extra strain has to be figured into the boat's service duty. As a consequence, I selected ½-inch thickness for the Surf Scoter's hull, but with an extra layer of ¼-inch plywood cold-molded to the bottom for a total thickness of ¾ inch.

Bulkhead placement is important, too. Keep the maximum unreinforced area of skin between bulkheads, stringers, and other primary structures to no more than 12 square feet.

In my designs, I use several types of rigid-clamp support systems at the sheer. The sheer clamp provides a strong, stiff, and fair curve up at the edge of the hull. In

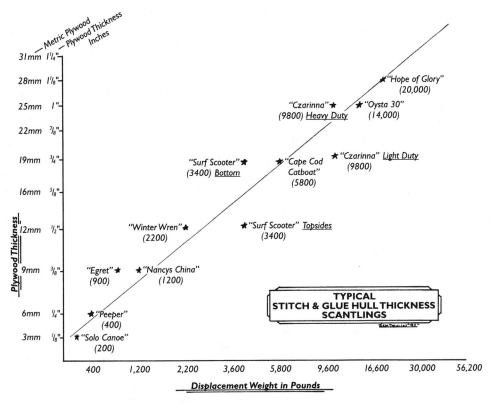

Figure 10-5. Plywood skin thickness varies according to displacement.

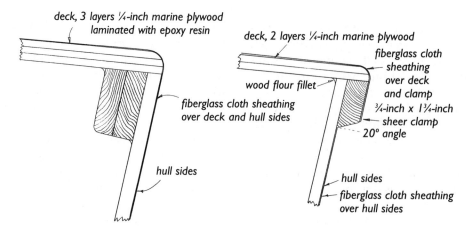

deck, 3 layers ¼-inch marine plywood
laminated with epoxy resin

deck, 2 layers ¼-inch marine plywood

fiberglass cloth
sheathing
over deck
and clamp

wood flour fillet

fiberglass cloth sheathing
over deck and hull sides

¾-inch x 1¾-inch
sheer clamp

20° angle

hull sides

hull sides

fiberglass cloth sheathing
over hull sides

*Figure 10-6. External, right, and internal sheer clamp arrangements. The
internal sheer clamp arrangement is often used for larger boats.*

the initial building stages of stitch-and-glue construction, the sheerline is defined only by spreaders or by bulkheads, and it can look a bit scalloped. A laminated sheer clamp stiffens and helps hold the span between the bulkheads fair. Later, the clamp will also serve nicely as the landing and fastening point for athwartships deck beams and ultimately for the deck. By notching the sheer clamp member, you can let in the prelaminated or sawn-to-shape deck beams.

A better arrangement uses longitudinal deck and cabin beams and eliminates the athwartship beams. This makes sense,

since the middle of the belowdecks area, especially in a small boat, gets the heaviest fore-and-aft traffic flow. If you have minimal headroom, athwartship beams mean more head-knockers. In contrast, a couple of stiff longitudinal beams allow you to leave the center 20 to 28 inches uncluttered, with maximum headroom. If carefully planned and crafted, longitudinal beams look just as proper in their supporting role as would athwartships beams. Furthermore, fairing the deck or cabintop lines is made easier since there are fewer parts to fit.

In either construction, the sheer clamps/stringers serve as strong landing

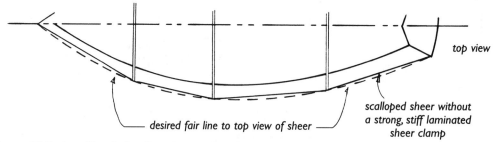

top view

desired fair line to top view of sheer

scalloped sheer without
a strong, stiff laminated
sheer clamp

*Figure 10-7. A scalloped sheerline. A strong, stiff laminated sheer stiffener
or clamp fairs between hard spots caused by spreaders or bulkheads.*

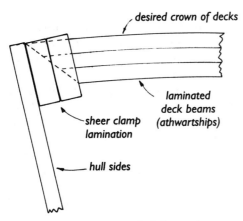

Figure 10-8. *Notching of deck beams into a sheer clamp.*

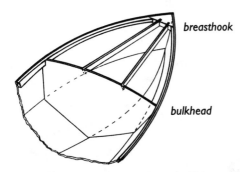

Figure 10-9. *A bow view of Nancy's China, with longitudinal deck beams let into a breasthook forward and bulkhead aft.*

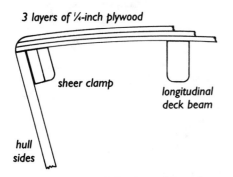

Figure 10-10. *A deck laminated from layers of thin plywood over framing.*

points for the deck. A sailboat has the additional strain of its rig to contend with, but in all boats, dock rash, bumps, scrapes, gouges, bashes, and miscellaneous insults all seem to focus on the sheer and hull-to-deck joint—about 70 to 90 percent of a boat's wear and tear, in fact. A strong sheer clamp heavily reinforces and protects this area.

Decks and cabintops are also subject to heavy stress, so don't be tempted to make the decks too light. Just imagine a clumsy, overweight oaf jumping from a high fuel dock onto your deck. Laminate the decks over the deck framing with several layers of thin plywood. Laminated decks help tie the deck framing to the sheer clamp, which in turn is tied to the sides of the hull. A laminated deck acts as a huge breasthook or knee. I've found that a ½- to ¾-inch laminate usually is a reasonable compromise between adequate stiffness and excessive weight.

Stitch-and-glue boats use taped and filleted seams to both hold the hull together and bond the rest of the internal structure. As a rule of thumb, I strive for a joint that is

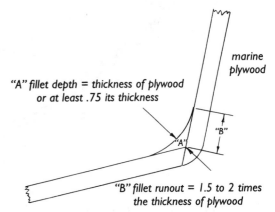

Figure 10-11. *Approximate fillet dimensions for stitch-and-glue joints.*

as strong as the pieces it bonds—but no stronger.

If we could meet that specification every time it would be perfect engineering. Some say that L. Francis Herreshoff's design for a turnbuckle was so perfect that when strength-tested, no one part failed before the other. Failure occurred virtually simultaneously in every part. That is my ideal for a stitch-and-glue boat. Tailor fillet thicknesses and weights and widths of glass cloth reinforcing to achieve uniform strengths. A fillet's minimum depth should be equal to the thickness—or at least 75 percent of the thickness—of the plywood being bonded.

For example, a dinghy or small rowing skiff constructed of ¼-inch plywood skin should have a fillet about ¼ inch deep. The runout of the fillet (the B dimension in Figure 10-11) should be double the thickness of the plywood, or ½ inch from the joint's center in this instance. This fillet helps to smoothly transfer the strength

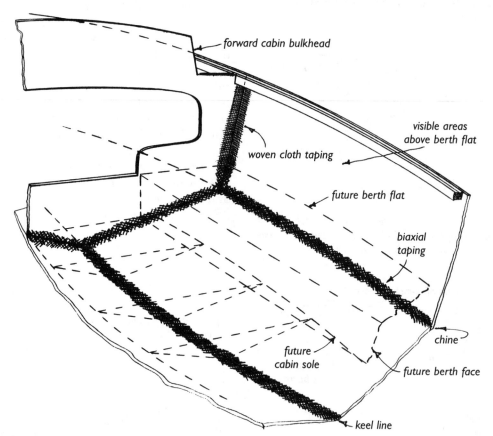

Figure 10-12. A view of the forward cabin bulkhead Arctic Tern 23-foot sloop. Biaxial tapes are used in hull seams while woven cloth taping is used where seams will be visible on finished boat.

from one panel to another without an abrupt interface. Layers of fiberglass tape over the fillet should be tapered, allowing the fabric to strengthen the joint while gradually distributing loads and avoiding stress concentrations. In the case of the skiff, 3- and 4-inch-wide, 6-ounce cloth layers would be more than adequate. Do your primary reinforcement of the hull seams and the bulkhead and hull joints on the interior for easier smoothing and to avoid unsightly bulging exterior seams.

On smaller boats, Volan-finished, 6- or 8-ounce fiberglass cloth cut into tapes make strong, light joints. On larger boats, I use biaxial fiberglass cloth tapes for joint reinforcement. By planning ahead and knowing which areas will be finished bright, you can use woven cloth tapes in multiple layers for the visible areas rather than the off-colored biaxials. Use biaxial cloths for major hull joints however, since they are significantly stronger, and usually hidden in the finished boat.

A typical fillet in a 30-foot boat with a skin thickness of ¾ inch would be ¾-inch deep, on top of which you would align 6-, 8-, and 10 inch-wide laminations of biaxial cloth tapes. On top of that, a 12-inch-wide layer of 6-ounce glass cloth will help smooth the roughness of the biaxial tape and allow you to fair and sand without cutting into the biaxial tapes.

Stitch-and-glue construction is different from traditional plywood construction in the bilge or keel areas, which require a slight rabbet joint in the keel to attach the plywood skin to the boat's backbone and framework. In the stitch-and-glue boat, keels, skegs, and all other appendages should be bonded into place over the one-piece glass/epoxy sheathed hull to assure the hull's integrity.

It is difficult if not impossible to encapsulate and seal heavy, thick chunks of wood effectively with epoxy. If moisture is allowed into the wood, the wood's dimensions will change as it swells and contracts with varying temperatures and with changes in the moisture content of the wood. This dimensional instability results in incredible strain in the epoxy joints,

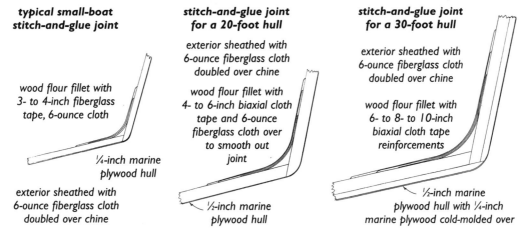

typical small-boat stitch-and-glue joint

wood flour fillet with 3- to 4-inch fiberglass tape, 6-ounce cloth

¼-inch marine plywood hull

exterior sheathed with 6-ounce fiberglass cloth doubled over chine

stitch-and-glue joint for a 20-foot hull

exterior sheathed with 6-ounce fiberglass cloth doubled over chine

wood flour fillet with 4- to 6-inch biaxial cloth tape and 6-ounce fiberglass cloth over to smooth out joint

½-inch marine plywood hull

stitch-and-glue joint for a 30-foot hull

exterior sheathed with 6-ounce fiberglass cloth doubled over chine

wood flour fillet with 6- to 8- to 10-inch biaxial cloth tape reinforcements

½-inch marine plywood hull with ¼-inch marine plywood cold-molded over

Figure 10-13. Stitch-and-glue chine joints vary according to the size of the boat.

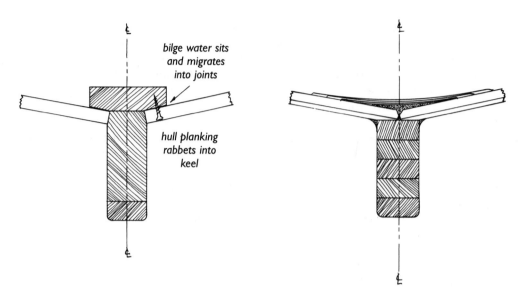

Figure 10-14. A keel of traditional plywood construction, left, and one of multiple laminations of ¾-inch material.

which ultimately can lead to failure. The larger the piece of wood, the greater the dimensional change it undergoes. In general, I'd say that no piece of wood thicker than ¾ inch can be adequately sealed with epoxy. If you have a thick keel to build, laminate many layers of thin stock. If you pre-fer to use thick dimensional stock, attach it to the hull so it won't tear the boat apart if it does change shape. I build a hull so its structural integrity is not compromised by problems with the stem or keel. To me, these parts are replaceable, but even so, they must be copiously sealed with epoxy.

11

BUILDING CRADLES

In virtually every form of boatbuilding, from traditional wood to modern fiberglass, aluminum, and steel, the builder must provide some form of backbone framework or complicated mold around which the boat is built. Only with stitch-and-glue, Scandinavian lapstrake, and dugout canoe construction can one avoid molds and frameworks.

No true stitch-and-glue design requires any form of backbone framework or mold.

There are, however, many stitch-and-glue variations that require some form of integral building mold. Phil Bolger and Dynamite Payson's tack-and-tape designs, for example, use precut bulkheads over which skin panels are assembled. As time passes we'll probably see other quasi stitch-and-glue methods that use integral bulkhead framing over which hulls are assembled upside down. That's just fine, since the method would still take advantage of composite stitch-and-glue joints—and if a partial mold makes sense or makes the job easier, I'm all for it. Most of my designs don't require assembly frameworks and are true stitch-and-glue designs, with the shapes of the panels dictating the final shape of the hull, assembled rightside up, then rolled over for bottom work when the interior is glassed.

With larger designs, the builder must provide a cradle, but only to help keep the hull level and the panels in proximate relationship while they are wired. The cradle supports the hull when the builder must climb in to install bulkheads and other structures, and it keeps the panels from flexing out of their true relationship with one another. One alternative to a cradle is a set of wooden blocks, sawhorses, or boatyard-type jackstands. Jackstands, in particular, are fairly inexpensive and effective, and are what I use in my shop. But if you cannot reach the centerline of your boat without climbing into it, it's easiest to build a simple cradle to efficiently work in the interior. If the boat is large enough to require this, it probably also needs support for transport and launching, and if you prefer to not use a trailer, the cradle could double as support for transport as well as maintenance and storage. The cradle I built for my Arctic Tern is still in fine shape after eight years of constant use.

A cradle's most important purpose,

Figure 11-1. Jackstands support the stern of the 29-foot Means of Grace. The chains prevent the jackstands from spreading apart.

Figure 11-2. A simple building cradle, which can be used for launching the boat as well as winter storage.

however, is to keep the boat level and square, especially when filleting and glassing the interior joints. Once cradled, it is immeasurably easier to level the boat longitudinally and athwartships. During every stage of building, it is important to keep checking the levelness of the hull struc-ture; failure to keep it level will quickly lead to the misplacement, misalignment, or even twisting of interior structures and a ruined hull.

I prefer a cradle that uses longitudinal beams as skids for the base, built up with crossmembers that touch and support the

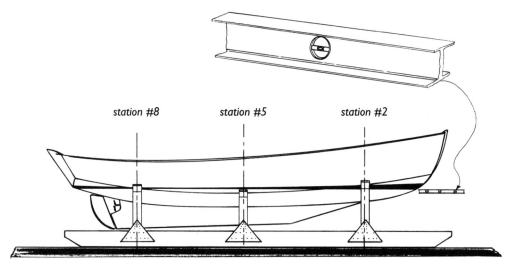

Figure 11-3. Leveling a building cradle.

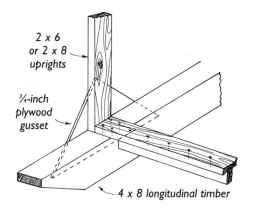

2 x 6
or 2 x 8
uprights

¾-inch
plywood
gusset

4 x 8 longitudinal timber

Figure 11-4A. Cradle support system.

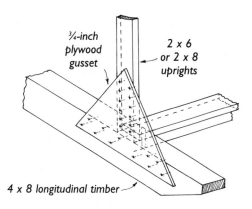

¾-inch
plywood
gusset

2 x 6
or 2 x 8
uprights

4 x 8 longitudinal timber

Figure 11-4B. Reverse view.

hulls at stations 2, 5, and 8, based on a 10-station plan. If your plan does not specify the cradle dimension details, you can easily figure out the cradle points from the station lines of your design.

To build a cradle for a boat under 14 feet long, use 2- x 6-inch skids and 2- x 4-inch crossmembers and uprights. When making cradles for larger boats (up to 32 feet), I use 4- x 8-inch skids and 2- x 8-inch crossmembers and uprights.

Align the skid members first. Determine the width of the truck or flatbed trailer you'll be using to move and launch the boat. My flatbed is 5 feet 8 inches between the rails, so the skids on all my cradles are just a bit narrower than that. Build up the cross rails at the 2/5/8 station intervals and appropriate angles and lengths. The metal joist brackets available at lumberyards are perfect for attaching and stabilizing the crossmembers, or you can make scrap plywood gussets to reinforce the cradle.

Place the uprights on top of the cross rails. If you are building a keel boat, build the uprights in two sections so they support the hull port and starboard, leaving

sufficient room for the keel. On larger keel boats, you might want to build two sets of uprights, one for the hull in a low (keel-less) position, and one for the hull with the keel in place, since much of the interior work is accomplished before the hull is

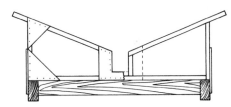

Figure 11-5A. End view of building cradle for a powerboat hull.

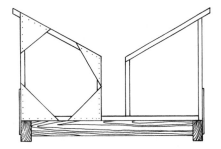

Figure 11-5B. Notched building cradle for the keel of a sailboat.

rolled over for exterior glassing and keel attachment. The lower uprights will make interior work easier by eliminating the additional climbing that would otherwise be necessary.

Reinforce all of the potentially moveable joints in the cradle structure with plywood gussets. Protect the cradle surfaces that will come into contact with the hull with layers of scrap carpet padding, nailing or stapling the padding along the sides of or underneath the uprights to prevent nail heads from damaging the boat. Use a good exterior-grade house paint to protect all exposed cradle surfaces from weathering during outdoor storage. Built this way, your cradle can live a long and useful life.

For really big boats—32 feet and larger—you will have to increase the sizes of your cradle timbers substantially. Use your own judgment and remember it is quite likely this cradle will live alongside the boat for a long time. It's worth doing a good job building it.

12

STITCHING UP THE HULL

This stage of the construction process involves stitching together the boat's panels using short pieces of steel wire. Unless you're building a really big boat, this is usually done while the hull is rightside up. This is the heart and soul of the stitch-and-glue construction technique, and what separates it from all other methods of building a wooden boat. The stitching process allows us to build a boat with no building molds or framework, and it permits at least a 30 percent reduction in hull construction labor relative to any other one-off construction method.

The wire stitches clamp together the large "peels" of the stitch-and-glue boat until epoxy composite joints can be applied, welding together the plywood panels of the boat into its final form.

Since no real forms or building molds are used, the stitching phase is a critical step. We'll use a simple V-bottomed single-

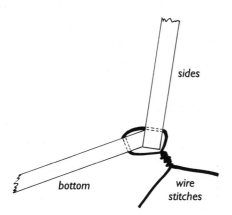

Figure 12-1. Side panels project down past bottom panels.

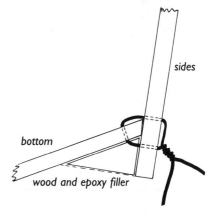

Figure 12-2. For high-speed powerboats, sides should extend even farther past bottom panels to accommodate chine flat.

chine hull to illustrate the process.

A couple of basics: First, I always over-lap the side panels down past the bottom panels, thus allowing the lofted chine edge or curve of the bottom panels to define the true chine of the boat. This method also allows the side panels to protrude below the chine of a high-speed powerboat that requires a built-in chine strip or flat. I also feel that stitching is easier and the results are more fair when the sides overlap the bottom panels, because the side-panel ends can be sprung in and out and shifted up and down to adjust to the bottom pan-els as you stitch.

Begin by laying out the two bottom panels, interior face to interior face, on the floor or on sawhorses. While these panels are clamped together, scribe a stitch line that follows their keel edges but is set back by the thickness of the plywood plus ⅛ inch. For example, if the plywood is ½-inch thick, the stitch line must be ⅝ inch away from the edges. Using the scribe line along the keel as a sewing line, drill a series of holes about 6 inches apart along the length of the keel edge, through both pan-els. Within 2 to 4 feet of each end, where the greatest stress occurs on the stitching,

drill the holes every 2 inches. Make sure the holes are perpendicular to the ply-wood surfaces. Next separate the two pan-els and bevel their inside keel edges sepa-rately, using a block plane or router set at 45 degrees. Bevel only to the halfway point of the plywood's thickness. If you were to attempt to align the panels without the bevel, you'd find that the keel edges would overlap or one panel might ride up or down alongside the other panel. In either case, the resulting keel line would be unfair. The bevels give us friction to the joint, allowing us to hold proper align-ment more easily.

Prepare your wire stitching kit ahead of time. Use a tray or bucket with compart-ments for pre-cut 6-inch lengths of steel wire, a sturdy pair of lineman's pliers, a drill with a ⅛-inch bit, and a small hammer. You may want to ask a friend to assist you in the stitching process.

After the panels are drilled, set them on sawhorses with the 45-degree beveled faces meeting and facing inward. If aligned correctly, the drilled holes will line up since the mating panels were drilled one on top of the other. Starting at the bow end, thread the wires individually through

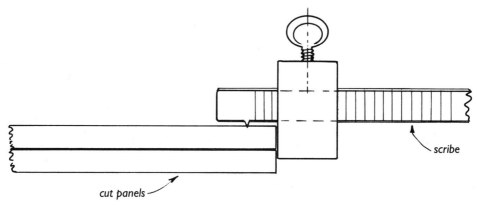

Figure 12-3. Scribing a stitch line on plywood.

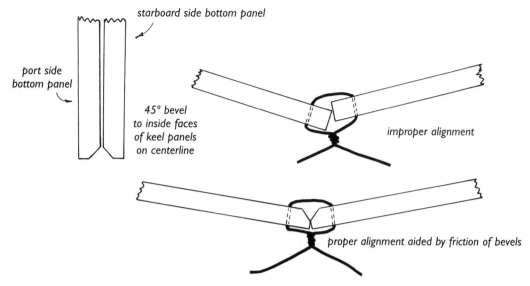

port side bottom panel

starboard side bottom panel

45° bevel
to inside faces
of keel panels
on centerline

improper alignment

proper alignment aided by friction of bevels

Figure 12-4. Beveling is essential for proper alignment of bottom panels.

the holes, twisting them to snug up the panels. Work your way toward the stern, stitching the keel line seam. If necessary, use a dowel the same diameter as the plywood thickness to twist the wires over. After breaking a handful of wires or tearing out a few holes you will learn how snug you can

tighten the wires. The wire stitches should have enough slack to allow the bottom panels to spread and still fit snugly. If the

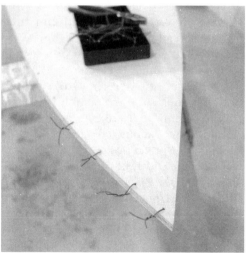

Figure 12-6. Wire stitches in place on the book-folded bottom panels. Note the bevels on the inboard edges of the panels and the tautness of the wire twists.

Figure 12-5. The stitching kit: tray, precut wire sutures, lineman's pliers, and a drill motor.

85

Figure 12-7. A dowel or pencil the approximate thickness of the plywood will act as a form around which to twist the wire stitches.

stitches are too tight, the bottom panels will not spread properly, and if they're too loose, you'll get a sloppy and poor fitting seam with an unfair keel line.

Move the stitched (but still stacked) bottom panels to your assembly area, and spread them open like a book. They should open to about 160 degrees. To hold them in the spread position, cut a piece of wood to the width of one bottom panel. This is the *bottom spreader*. Keeping this spreader horizontal, attach it with a loop of rope or wire around its midpoint to any wire stitch in the keel line, then tighten the loop by twisting it with a stick to pull down the spreader until the correct bottom positioning is realized. This method is particularly useful to someone working alone.

Once the bottom panels are posi-

Figure 12-8. With the bottom panels stitched along the keel line, they can be spread open.

Figure 12-9. On a larger stitch-and-glue hull the panels must be spread gently to avoid tearing stitches or plywood edges.

tioned and spread, bevel the outside chine edges with a block plane. This is also the time to contend with the *transition joint,* which is unnecessary in flat-bottomed or shallow V-bottomed boats, but is required

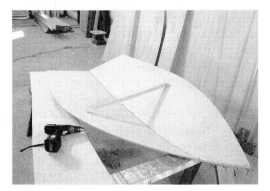

Figure 12-10. A batten can help spread the bottom panels prior to stitching the sides.

to smooth the bow portion of the chine of boats in which the V-shape is pronounced.

A short explanation of this transition joint is in order. The chine, of course, is the intersection of the bottom panels with the side panels. During the wiring process, the side panels overlap the edge of the bottom panels. As the panels are pulled together, they have the freedom to curve fairly into the boat's profile. But in the bow sections, the deadrise angle of the bottom panels increases, and the chine angle between bottom and side panels gets progressively larger, until it is no longer feasible for the side panel to overlap the bottom panel. At this point (just aft of the stem/chine intersection), in order to achieve a fair chine curve and avoid an obvious overbite of the stem in the profile, we make a shift in the seam from a lap

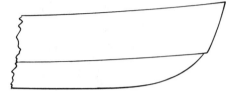

Figure 12-11. With no transition joint, the stem shows an overbite.

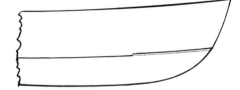

Figure 12-12. Stem profile with an adequate transition joint.

joint to a butt joint. This is done by cutting a notch in the forward end of the side panel to compensate for the abrupt change of the chine as it fairs up with the side panel into the stem. Your plans should indicate the length of the transition joint for the design you are building. I generally use 12- to 18-inch transition joint lengths for boats up to 10 feet long, 24 inches for boats 11 to 17 feet long, 36 inches for boats 18 to 25 feet long, and 48 inches for boats 26 to 40 feet long. The only objective of these transition joints is to allow the panels to join more fairly the entire length of the boat.

Begin setting up a transition joint by marking and cutting a notch the specified transition length from the forward chine of the side panels. I cut the notch deep enough to match the thickness of the plywood bottom panels plus ⅛ inch, which should allow us enough height to keep the transition joint fair.

Next, after the two bottom halves have been stitched along the keel line and spread, but before planing the chine edge, go to the forward end of the bottom panels. Measure back from the stem intersection the length of the notch that was previously cut from the side panels, and mark it on the bottom panels. With a handsaw, make a small cut on that mark at the approximate angle at which the side panel bears to the bottom panel in the transition area.

Now go to the stern end of the bottom panels and plane the entire chine edge up to the saw cut, but not past it; this is the point at which the side panel changes from running down alongside the bottom panels to jumping up and abutting the bottom panels as in the illustrations. Make sure to plane only to the cut upper edge of the bottom panels; any farther and you would radically change the design.

Next, lay the two side panels face to face, making sure they are on a completely flat surface. Scribe a line along the chine edge of the panels just as you scribed a line along the keel edge of the bottom panels, ⅛ inch plus the thickness of the plywood from the edge. While the panels are clamped together, drill the stitching holes about 4 inches apart. Within 24 to 48 inches of the panel ends, where the greatest strains will occur, drill the holes 2 inches apart. I always drill as many holes as I think might be necessary in the worst case to stitch up the boat. While stitching the panels you may find that you don't need wire ties in all the holes; even so, the predrilled holes serve as a guide during the stitching process, and it's a lot easier to drill holes accurately when the panels are flat. By drilling both side panels simultaneously, there is symmetry to the stitches. Separate the two side panels, and bevel a 45-degree angle on the inside of the stem edge of both panels to aid alignment

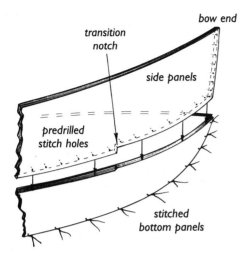

Figure 12-13. Transition joint details.

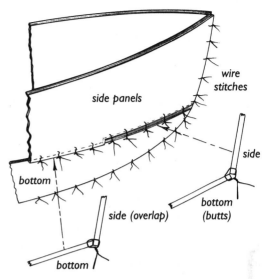

Figure 12-14. Transition joint stitching details.

there, just as you did on the keel edges of the bottom panels.

At this point we have predrilled holes in the chine edges of the side panels, but not in the chine edges of the bottom panels. I wait to drill those holes until I am actually starting to stitch on the side panels. That way I can easily align hole locations and clamp the hull panels more accurately. Drill only one or two holes at a time in the bottom panels, setting them back from the edge by about the thickness of the plywood. The easiest way to wire the chine lines is to push the wire into the predrilled side panel hole from the outside, bend it into a U-shape, and return it through the freshly drilled mating hole in the bottom panel. Drill only a few holes at a time in the bottom panel, directly opposite the side panel holes, and stitch as you go along each side. Start stitching the side panels from the bow end first. As you move toward the stern, set and tighten the wires, trying to set up each stitch with even tightness and force.

If you are right-handed, start with the starboard side panel at the bow. Leaning

over the side, you should be able to drill holes in the bottom panel to ensure that the hole is opposite the predrilled hole in the side panel. If you have a helper, have that person hold the end of the side panel in

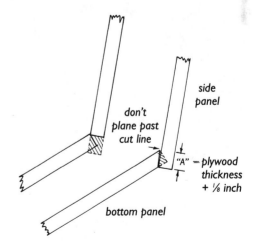

Figure 12-15. Notch height of transition joint cut in chine edge of side panel.

alignment. And with simple guidance from the stitcher they can move the panel up or down or in and out to allow for good alignment. If you are working alone, and the boat is quite large, you may need to suspend the panel from a rafter or clamp a board to the end to brace the panel from the floor. Either way, with adjustments to suspension or to the brace, you should be able to stitch together the panels. Complete one entire side before moving to the other side. When attaching the port side panel, again work from stem to stern. You might find it helpful to fasten several wires at the top of the stem line just to hold the two side panels upright and in proper alignment while stitching up the rest of the chine.

Constantly check the fairness of the seam throughout the process. All the wires should enter the side panel flush with the top edge of the bottom panel; if not you will have a loose or unfair chine line. When you twist the wires snug, make them uniformly tight.

After both sides are stitched, fully wire the stem line from bottom to top, making sure to maintain side-to-side alignment and the symmetry of the bow. Then secure the transom, wiring or using nails or screws to position it. Your hull is now stitched up but still in a somewhat misshapen form that we'll cover in the next chapter.

A few notes about stitching: I have learned the hard way that ultimately no part of the wire should be left in the stitch points in the finished boat. As much as you might think it would be easier to simply trim the stitching flush with the panel surfaces and glass over, beware! All metals contract and expand at different rates than

Figure 12-16. Side panel stitching on a larger design. The hull is large enough to allow the interior boatbuilder to drill and poke wire stitches through to the outside, where they are twisted snug. The worker to the right adjusts the side panel for proper alignment.

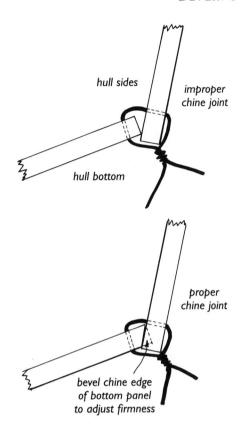

hull sides

improper chine joint

hull bottom

proper chine joint

bevel chine edge
of bottom panel
to adjust firmness

Figure 12-17. Proper and improper alignment of side and bottom panels.

wood and epoxy, and sooner or later, these wire remnants will work their way out through the surface of your paint and finish. I use mild steel wire (16 gauge) for my stitching because of that. Steel wire is tough enough to hold your panels together, yet can be extracted fairly easily. Baling wire purchased from a local hardware store is cheap, easy to use, and readily available. On some larger boats, though, I have found that baling wire is not consistently strong enough to hold the big, stiffer panels. For those boats, galvanized electric fence wire (12.5 or 14 gauge) is the cheapest and best alternative. You can buy it from a feed store in large spools. Try it; I think it works great.

Considering all the ideas being bandied about, stitching seems to be a fascinating process that has captivated many good minds in search of ways to make it easier. And while any good idea on fastening panels is fine with me, the point is, the stitching process is easy. Go ahead and use monofilament fish line, or nylon cable ties, or staples, nails, or anything else. Just make sure that you can get those stitches out of the seam before the boat's finished.

Wire stitch removal is covered in Chapter 16, but a hint of what to expect will be useful here. There are two choices for removing the wires from the joints, and I use either depending on my work schedule and the size of the boat. The first is to place small epoxy fillets between each wire stitch on the interior seams with a fast-curing thickened epoxy resin. When those fillets cure, pull out the bulk of the wire ties, leaving in just a few in the high-stress areas of the hull.

Your other option is to fillet and tape completely all the seams, disregarding the wire stitching. When the epoxy cures, remove the wire stitches by applying enough heat to the wire to cause the epoxy to release its tenacious hold on the metal, and pull the wire out of the joints with a set of pliers. Either way works fine and shouldn't be a problem.

13

BULKHEADS, CLAMPS, AND FLOOR TIMBERS

BULKHEADS

Although a stitch-and-glue boat primarily starts with the hull skin and works inward, it must also rely on interior structures for additional hull support. The simple dinghy gets support from seat thwarts, stern knees, breasthooks, and gunwales. In a large boat, a complicated grid of athwartships (sideways, or perpendicular to the centerline) and longitudinal (lengthwise, or parallel to the centerline)

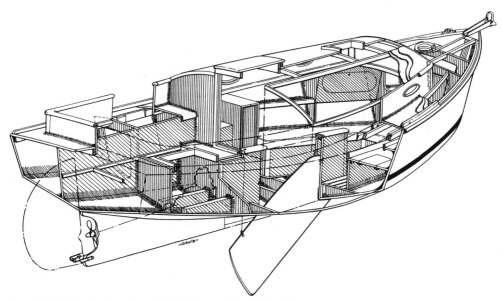

Figure 13-1. Perspective view of a 22-foot catboat built with stitch-and-glue construction. Every component serves a structural function. (Stephen L. Davis)

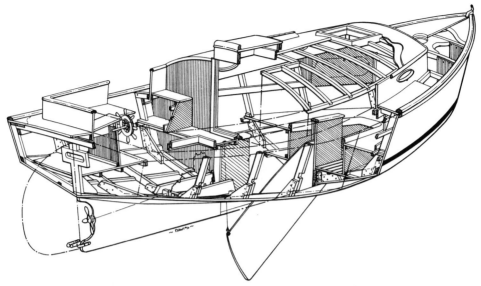

Figure 13-1A. View of the same 22-foot catboat, built using traditional construction methods. Note additional framing. (Stephen L. Davis)

bulkheads provides this critical support. These bulkheads need to be fitted into place, and bonded with the same type of epoxy fillet/fiberglass tape seams that hold the hull panels together. Great care must be exercised to ensure that the bulkheads are located with precision and in proper relationship to the sheerline and waterline of the boat.

If you are building a sizable boat, before you can turn the boat upside down for exterior sheathing, you will need to reinforce and stiffen it by installing a few of the major athwartships bulkheads. You need not install longitudinal bulkheads yet (see Chapter 23), nor need you install *all* the athwartships bulkheads at this time; you can postpone some of this work if you wish. But the major athwartships bulkheads should go in now. Not only do they reinforce and stiffen the hull, but these thick bulkheads may receive fastenings

through the hull sides, and you want the heads of those fastenings to be sealed by the exterior sheathing or by exterior cold-molding. The smaller the boat, the less likely are the bulkheads to receive through-hull fastenings, and the less necessary they are to stiffen the hull prior to turning it upside down. So there is judgment involved in deciding how much of the bulkhead grid you need to install now and how much will keep until later. On my designs, I often label bulkheads according to their recommended time of installation: those necessary to install before rollover and those that can wait for later installation. If your plans don't include this information, better to err on the safe side and bond in those major bulkheads nearest to stations #2, #5, and #8 as soon as possible.

Before starting the seams, you'll need to adjust and level the stitched-together hull. If you are correctly aligned to the

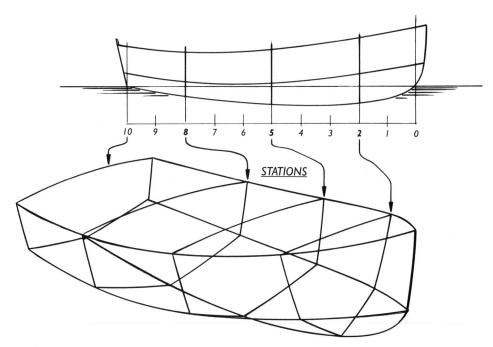

Figure 13-2. Position major support bulkheads as near as possible to stations #2, #5, and #8.

designed waterline, you will be level in both the longitudinal (fore and aft) and athwartships (lateral) orientations. If your hull is out of level, the bulkheads may not contact in the locations shown on the plans.

Most stitch-and-glue plans will show a lengthwise scale or ruling line marked with athwartships hull bulkhead positions. Your hull must be positioned properly, with sheer beams or spreaders in place (see Chapter 12) to set up the correct design shape. If your sheer spreaders are too wide or narrow, your hull will be misshapen. As you spread the hull to its proper beam the bow will rise or fall, and as a result the athwartships bulkhead positions, which are measured aft from the bow, will change. Therefore, go through each major bulk-

Figure 13-3. The difference between this boat's bow and stern freeboard is 8 inches. Measuring from the transom edges and the bow to your shop floor or some other level surface should produce the same difference.

Figure 13-4. The boatstands under the stern of this 29-foot Black Crown powerboat can adjust for the twist of the large transom. The Black Crown is multichined, and the upper side panel has not yet been attached. Note the spreaders, which will be used at both the intermediate and the upper sheer.

head, spreading the hull beam to its proper width as you move aft from the stem, to double-check its location and its athwartships beam, or width.

After sheer spreaders are positioned at each major bulkhead station and the hull has been spread at the sheer to its proper beam, you are ready to verify the bulkhead information. *This is very important: Even if your designer has given dimensions and sizes for all bulkheads, double-check the bulkhead dimensions anyway.* The characteristics of plywood differ, and hull panels can bend differently boat to boat. It's easy to check, and this will avoid a lot of grief later on.

For example, my shop has built two Surf Scoters side by side, with one hull stitched of 7-ply, 12mm plywood and the other stitched of 5-ply, 12mm plywood. The bulkhead dimensions ended up slightly different because the 7-ply hull stock was stiffer, and the relationship between these hull panels differed from the interaction of the more flexible 5-ply boat and panels. The differences were most noticeable in the bow and stern sections: Stiffer wood means less shape, more flexible wood means more shaping ability, so you may need to adjust the bulkheads accordingly. If your bulkhead sizes differ dramatically from the plan, however, you should stop and review all your prior steps for accuracy, checking particularly that the hull setup is level and there is no twisting in the hull.

You will also need to check your stitched-up hull for longitudinal twisting. The best check is to measure back diagonally from the tip of the stem to each top corner of the transom. If your transom had been screwed or stitched in place symmetrically, that diagonal measurement should be exactly the same port and starboard. If it varies you most probably have a hull that is somewhat twisted. It's easy to adjust this by placing small legs under the transom and wedging until the diagonal measurement is the same. A final check with a Smartlevel, spirit level, or water level will give you the confidence that your hull is true.

If your hull flexes and moves too much when you are climbing about checking bulkhead measurements, you can always tab areas of the chine and keel with a bit of wood flour and epoxy. This stiffens the boat and allows you to work with fewer flexing problems. Place the tabs from 8 to 12 inches apart along the chine lines and keel lines. Be careful not to place tabs in the way of the intersections of the bulkhead positions, as that only makes your measuring job that much more difficult.

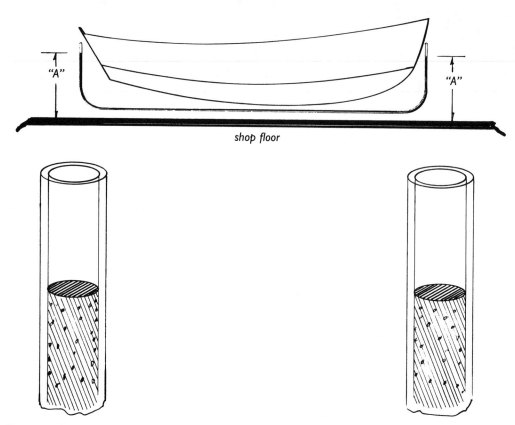

Figure 13-5. Waterhose leveling of a hull. Use clear vinyl hose.

To verify each bulkhead position, stretch a tape measure from the stem along the centerline of the boat, then lay a batten from sheer to sheer at the bulkhead location, perpendicular to the tape measure. Lightly mark the front edge of the batten where it intersects the sheer both port and starboard, along the tops of the plywood side panels where they intersect the batten. Now hook the end of your tape measure over the stem centerline of the hull and move the tape side to side, measuring the diagonals to each of the marked bulkhead ends. These two measurements should match. If they aren't the same and you are sure that the waterline and athwartship alignment is correct, your batten wasn't perpendicular to the centerline tape.

Adjust your batten by averaging between the port length and the starboard length. For example, if you measure 108¼ inches on the port diagonal and 109¼ inches on the starboard diagonal, you need to move the mark aft on the port side by half the difference, and forward half of the distance on the starboard side. In this case, the difference is 1 inch, so both sides will have to move ½ inch so they measure 108¾ inches on the diagonal from the stem. With the batten aligned to the new sheer markings, recheck the batten's half-beam measurement from the centerline to see whether it still matches the design's bulkhead sheer dimensions. If all these measurements check out, repeat the process at the next bulkhead station.

When building a multichined vessel such as the Black Crown, you must go through this measuring procedure not only at the sheer, but also at the tops of the lower side panels (also known as bilge panels). With the Black Crown, you'll note two

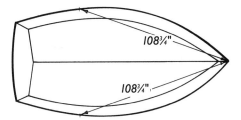

Figure 13-6. Bulkhead beam measurements.

sets of longitudinal measurements to the bulkhead positions, because the stem rakes forward approximately 2 inches from the top of the bilge panel to the top of the upper side panel (the true sheer). You'll also note two sets of measurements for the beam inside the planking, one for the top of the sheer panel and one for the top of the bilge panel.

Once all the major bulkhead positions are marked at the top of the side panels and the proper beams have been established at each bulkhead station with spreaders tacked in place, lay a straight, stiff batten from side to side on top of the sheer to intersect both sheer marks. Drop a plumb bob down and mark its intersection with the keel centerline and with each chine line. Then use a smaller straightedge to draw lines on the hull panels from the mark on the starboard sheer, to the starboard chine, and from the starboard chine to the centerline or keel mark. Repeat on the port side. These lines define the bulkhead placement, so you can quickly check your actual bulkhead dimensions against the designed dimensions. Using this easy method of locating and drawing in the bulkhead placements, you have the capability of positioning almost any piece of the boat in the hull shell, thereby quickly defining its actual shape.

Measure the bulkhead dimensions

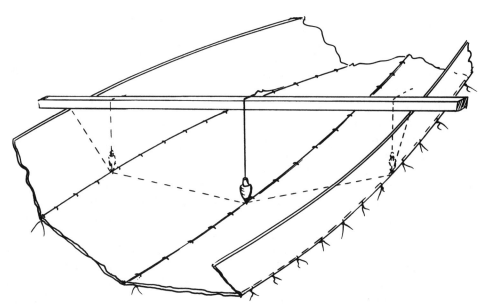

*Figure 13-7. Marking bulkhead locations using a plumb bob and a
stiff batten.*

from sheer to sheer (the width of the boat
inside the plywood sides), checking that it
matches the building plans exactly. This
width should not vary from your plans since
it was set up by you with spreaders. Next,
measure the inside width from chine to
chine, noting this dimension on the bulkhead sheet of the plans. Now measure down
perpendicular from the straightedge to the
chine, and then to the centerline of the
keel, in each case ensuring that you measure down from where the plumb bob
string was held to the batten. Compare the
two widths and two heights you have just
measured with the designed dimensions on
the plans. Though there may be some small
discrepancies due to the stiffness of the hull
planking, there should be no change in the
width at the sheer, since this dimension
comes from the spreaders you have put in
place. If the change of any of the "B," "C,"
or "D" measurements is dramatic, on the
order of 1 inch or more, double-check the
bulkhead placement and the levelness of
the hull to the designed waterline.

On some designs you might confront
an angled bulkhead. The approach for

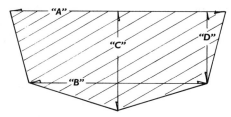

A: Width at sheer
   (as set by builder from plan dimensions).
B: Width at chine
   (as measured from stitched hull).
C: Depth from sheer to keel line
   (as measured from stitched hull).
D: Depth from sheer to chine
   (measured from stitched hull).

Figure 13-8. Key bulkhead dimensions.

these is similar, except that you will not be able to use a plumb bob for picking up the points on the chine and the keel. Instead, make up a large angle-gauge with a couple of straightedges and a C-clamp. Set your gauge to the designed bulkhead angle from the building plans, then lay a wide (approximately 10-inch) board on the flat from sheer to sheer, and lay your angle-gauge on that. Extending the leg of the angle-gauge with a clamped straightedge as necessary, mark the intersections at the chine and the keel. This locates the bulkhead on the hull panels. Check the resultant dimensions against the plans as for vertical bulkheads.

Another method of checking is to set up a Smartlevel and shoot down to chine/keel points at the proper angle.

When you are satisfied with your bulkhead measurements, draw in the bulkheads on your plywood stock. The plans may state the grain orientation and should note—if a bulkhead is wider than 4 feet or taller than 8 feet—where the butt joints should lie. (If your plans don't show that information, you can work it out on your own.) Mark the centerline of the bulkhead first, since the half-beam dimensions are taken from the centerline outward. Next, measure vertically from the base of the bulkhead to the heights (on the centerline) of the chine, sheer, and any other point that is to be noted. With a framing or drywall square, draw the necessary horizontal lines. Mark the half-beam at the chine on the horizontal chine line (mark both sides if you are laying out the full bulkhead), and repeat the process to locate the sheer half-beams. Now connect the centerline or keel depth mark to the chine and sheer marks. The bottom panels may have some outward curvature between the chine and the keel, particularly in the forward half of the hull. If so,

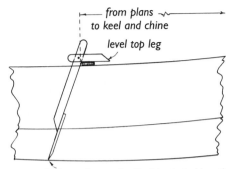

use small piece of scrap for final projected length

Figure 13-9. Bulkhead scribing. For angled bulkheads use a large bevel gauge made from scrap stock and shoot projections of the angle given in the plans from points at the sheer to the keel and chine.

lay a straightedge in the hull from keel to chine, measure the depth of the outward curvature, transfer and draw in that amount of curve on the bulkhead stock before you cut out the bulkhead. If you forget this step, you can fill in the gap later with epoxy resin and fillers. Draw in the deck camber between the sheer half-beam marks as described below.

Like the floor timbers (which we will install later), the bulkheads must be limbered to allow water to drain to a central low point in the bilge where it can be pumped out. I usually resist the temptation to compartmentalize any one area of the boat, and always give water an easy path to the bilge. The only exception is the engine box, which must be separate since it is neither legal nor environmentally sound to pump engine-related petroleum products overboard with bilge water. Isolating the engine compartment will contain fuel oil or lubricant spills until they can be cleaned up with oil soak rags or sponges and disposed of properly.

After cutting out the bulkhead, check for proper fit in the boat. You may want to

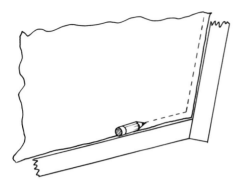

Figure 13-10. With a pencil laid flat (parallel) to the hull sides on bottom, mark a line on the bulkhead being fitted to produce a much sweeter fit.

scribe it into perfect position with this simple but accurate method: With your pencil laid flat on the hull panel and the bulkhead in place, draw a line around the perimeter of the bulkhead. This gives you a scribeline set back about ⅛ inch from the bulkhead edge. A bit of block plane work on the high spots outside the scribe line should allow the bulkhead to fit perfectly.

All the major bulkheads should be carefully measured and cut out before any interior taping is done on boats longer than 15 feet. Checking measurements for beams and heights and aligning these measurements to the designated plan dimensions will avoid miscutting of bulkheads and their adjacent parts. Before the bulkheads are installed, their edges and the contacting areas of the hull panels should be carefully sealed with epoxy. I usually coat the raw edges of the bulkheads first, then climb into the hull and coat the contacting areas on the hull panels. I then recoat the bulkhead edges, since the end grain of the plywood tends to absorb epoxy more readily. I place the bulkheads in the boat while the epoxy is still wet. Pin each

bulkhead in place with a few stainless steel sheet-metal screws (at least two or three per hull panel) through the panels and into the bulkhead edges. The screws will hold things in place until the epoxy sets up.

The bulkheads are then bonded into place with the same epoxy fillet and taped seam joints that bond the hull panels together. The process is the same: First coat the areas to be taped with unthickened epoxy resin to ensure there will be no resin starvation in the joint. Next apply the epoxy/wood flour fillet, and then apply the fiberglass tape layers using unthickened epoxy. I deal more extensively with glassing in Chapter 14.

On a larger boat, and always on one with a cabin, I fit all the major bulkheads in place before starting any seam taping on the hull panels or the bulkheads. It is much easier to check the dimensions of the bulkheads without having a filleted taped seam in the way, and your taping or glassing of the seams can be done in shorter, easier-to-handle segments after the major bulkheads are in place. I prefer to do the majority of the fitting in one session and the majority of the epoxy seam taping in one session. This makes less of a mess, and there is virtually no repeating of steps.

I also attempt to avoid installing bulkheads that extend much above the sheer of the boat at this stage. Remember, the initial hull stitch-up and bulkhead work is being done with the hull right side up. We want to add any interior structural members that will strengthen the hull prior to turning it over, but we don't want to add structures or parts that will make rolling the boat over more difficult to accomplish. Bulkheads that extend much past the sheer certainly do this. A good example is the Surf Scoter's aft pilothouse bulkhead, which extends almost 36 inches above the sheer. That means the boat would have to be blocked up an extra three feet while upside down for the exterior work.

The solution to bulkheads that extend significantly above the sheer can be to build the bulkhead in two halves—one from keel to sheer, and the second from the sheer up. Another solution is to install two bulkheads, one just in front of the other. In the Surf Scoter, a cockpit bulkhead between the keel and the sheer serves as a landing place for the cockpit sole and cockpit side decks. After rollover, the aft pilothouse bulkhead is added just in front of the cockpit bulkhead, providing a landing for the side decks of the boat. I fasten the two bulkheads together with screws, and build an epoxy/tape seam on the after side of the cockpit bulkhead and the forward side of the aft pilothouse bulkhead. This method is strong and easy, and provides landings for structures both in front of and behind the bulkheads.

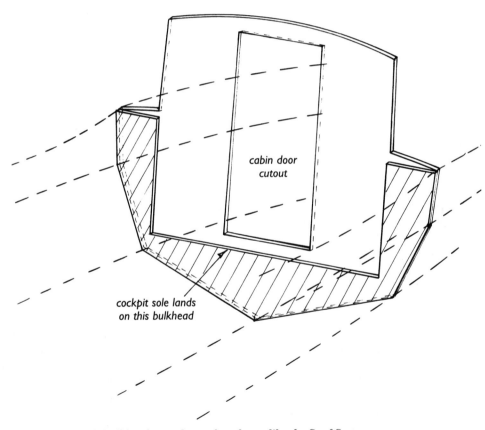

Figure 13-11. Double bulkheads can be used on boats like the Surf Scoter, whose high bulkheads make rollover and exterior sheathing inconvenient. The lower bulkhead (cross hatching) is installed before rollover, the higher section after sheathing.

STEP-BY-STEP SUMMARY OF BULKHEAD FITTING PROCEDURE

Level the stitched hull with the designed waterline.

Level the hull athwartships to the design waterline.

Mark the major bulkhead locations on the top of the sheer on both sides.

Lay a straightedge sideways across the boat, intersecting marks on sheer.

Drop a plumb bob to align vertical bulkheads and mark the bulkhead position at the chine or chines and at the keel centerline.

Measure the vertical distance (heights) from the straightedge to the chine and to the keel centerline at the locations marked in preceding step.

Measure the sheer and chine beams (widths) to the inside of planking.

Check these measurements against your plans, and correct the bulkhead dimensions as necessary on your plans.

When you are satisfied with your actual dimensions, lay out the plywood stock for the bulkheads.

For each bulkhead, draw in the centerline.

Mark the sheer height on the bulkhead centerline.

Mark the chine heights on the centerline.

Draw horizontal lines through the height marks, and along these mark off the half-beams at the sheer and chines.

Draw the deck camber as described below.

Draw in any other dimensions or details indicated on the plans.

Connect the dots and cut out the bulkhead.

Position the bulkheads in the boat and pencil-scribe to adjust into place as necessary.

Coat the edges of the bulkheads (and the hull where the bulkheads will land) with epoxy, and drop the bulkheads back into the hull, making sure the marks at the sheer, chines, and keel align to the proper side of the bulkhead (usually the aft side).

Pin each bulkhead into place with a minimum of two or three screws per hull panel. Screw holes can be pre-bored from inside the hull before final placement of the bulkhead to aid the positioning of the screws.

After all major bulkhead pieces are in place and the epoxy has cured, fillet and glass the hull-to-bulkhead joints.

DECK CAMBER

You will note on your plans that there is usually a deck camber called out, indicating the amount of crown in the deck. Typically this crown varies in height in relationship to the width of the boat at the point.

While the height varies according to width, note that both measurements in Figure 13-12 are taken along the same camber ruler. (Some designs may have complex camber, which varies along the length of the boat, but I find this a tedious and not very necessary detail, on decks in particular.) On my own designs I generally use a consistent camber ruler, or I revert to another method for establishing the camber, for example when a cabin top's forward crown differs from its aft crown.

There is a proper method to lay out for constant camber and a couple of easier methods. If you're a skilled draftsman,

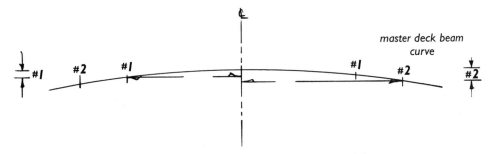

Figure 13-12. Deck camber ruler. Note the differences in the heights of the bulkhead crowns as the width of the beam changes.

you can loft it—or you can use this "cheater" method. Cut out two stiff, straight battens, each about 6 inches longer than the width of the boat. On a sheet or sheets of plywood, lay out a grid with a straight line equal to the maximun beam of the boat; this is your baseline. Drive a nail at each end of the baseline. At the baseline's midpoint, draw a perpendicular line and mark the overall height of the stated camber, driving a nail at that point. Now lay your two battens against the centerline nail and each baseline nail. Join the battens where they intersect with two

or more nails, then pull out the centerline nail. With a pencil in the crotch (see Figure 13-13) and the battens in full contact with the baseline nails, you can draw a true camber. Cut out the plywood pattern and use it as a tracing pattern on your bulkhead layouts—making sure the pattern's midpoint matches the centerline on the bulkhead.

SHEER CLAMPS

While the chines, keel line, and bulkheads can be easily bonded together with epoxy/

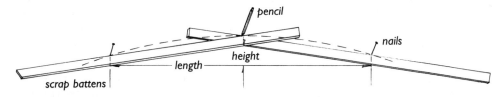

Figure 13-13. Beam/crown jigs.

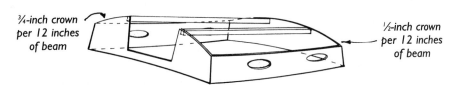

Figure 13-14. On a sailboat with forward and aft cabin bulkheads, use longitudinal cabintop beams to compensate for the differences between the two crowns.

taped seams, there isn't a convenient way to fasten the hull-to-deck joint (with composite glass/epoxy joints). Laminated sheer clamps provide stiff, fair landings for the decks. In open boats with unprotected sheers that are not braced to any other structure, it is important to reinforce that area with gunwale sheer clamps. All told there are several types of sheer clamps; we'll discuss the gunwale/clamp first.

Glued securely on the sheer of an open skiff, dinghy, or open rowing boat, a

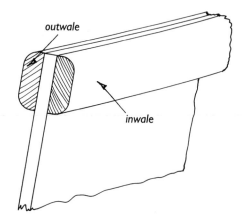

Figure 13-15A. Solid gunwale/clamp.

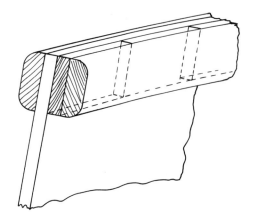

Figure 13-15B. Spacer blocks on the inwale of a gunwale/clamp.

gunwale/clamp looks good and finishes off the boat nicely. If the open boat is a sailing design or will be subject to a great amount of strain from oarlock fittings, I glue small spacer blocks to the sheer before fastening an inwale into place. This makes the inwale act as a girder and further stiffens the clamp.

The second type of sheer clamp is properly termed an exterior clamp, and it will stiffen and fair the sheer of a hull that has decks and bulkheads. While the chine is held fair in relationship to the bottom of the boat, the sheer is not. If there are bulkheads for interior structures, the sheer may actually stretch around the bulkheads, creating a somewhat scalloped look when viewed from above (see Figure 10-7). I don't often use an exterior clamp on boats longer than 24 feet, however, because it's hard to make a clamp structure with adequate support for the strains of a larger boat. The decks must fasten over the topside planking and the clamp, and when decks are sheathed, the cloth must wrap over and down onto the face of the exterior clamp. Unfortunately, because of the amount of glass that needs to be applied to reinforce this edge, it is difficult to bright-finish the sheer of the boat, as can easily be done when a gunwale clamp is used.

I use a variation of the exterior clamp on my Lichen design that incorporates a wider sheer clamp section, 4 inches wide and ¾ inch thick. To this I attach a smaller, ⅜-inch x 1-½-inch teak rubrail at the top of the sheer to finish off the joint and protect it from chafing wear.

A third type of clamp, for boats longer than 18 feet, is an interior clamp laminated from two or more layers of ¾-inch dimensional wood fastened through the topsides of the hull. Fasten the decks securely to the interior clamp and run the sheathing over the deck edge onto the topsides sheathing. A small hardwood rubrail can then be fastened at the sheer, just below the roundover at the deck edge, protecting the sheer from chafe. If you want toerails, they can be fastened over the deck into the clamp with long, countersunk screws.

Always install both port and starboard sheer clamps during the same work session. These clamps are stiff, and can pull a boat out of shape if the work isn't balanced side to side. Also try to run these clamps full length along the sheer, through notches in the bulkheads, so they will pull the plywood sheer into a fair curve. Often, I will laminate one layer at a time to make the clamp easier to handle, using C-clamps and fasteners to hold it in place until the epoxy sets up. I glue in a layer to port and one to starboard, clean up the excess glue, and the next day glue in the second layer, port then starboard.

Multichined vessels like the Surf Scoter use an intermediate sheer clamp system to pull the edge of the hull panels into fairness and to help reinforce the rest of the structure. After the hull bottom and bilge panels are wired, place spreaders or bulkheads inside the hull to push the proper beam shape into the upper edge of the bilge panels. Then laminate a sheer clamp into place with half its width extending above the top of the bilge panel. Plane off the excess wood to pick up the new angle of the upper side panel, or wale, and attach the wale by screwing through its bottom edge into the clamp. Unless it is so small as to allow rolling over by one or two persons, your hull will need the structural stiffness and reinforcement of the sheer clamps to avoid straining things when you roll it over.

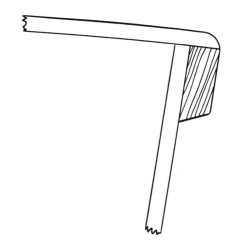

Figure 13-16A. Exterior gunwale/clamp for a small, decked boat.

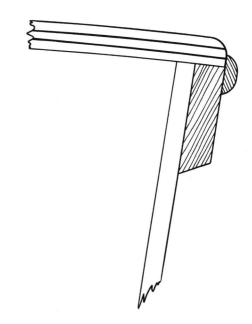

Figure 13-16B. Lichen-type exterior gunwale/clamp and guard.

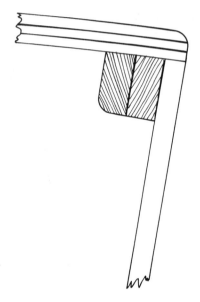

Figure 13-17A. Interior sheer clamp.

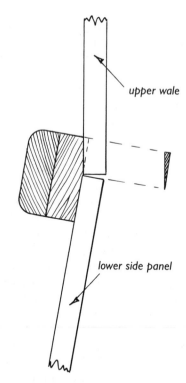

upper wale

lower side panel

Figure 13-18. Plane off the angle of top of intermediate clamp before attaching upper wale.

FLOOR TIMBERS

I prefer good, stout floor timbers built of a durable and stable wood—Honduras mahogany is best, but fir and yellow cedar are also good. Choose a wood that seals well with epoxy. (The bilge is going to have water in it some time or another, and your only recourse is to seal the holy heck out of it!)

Because of the odd shapes and the expense of the dimensional wood, I usually use templates made from thin scrap plywood to cut the floor timber stock. Templates speed up the work and save on materials.

Pick a starting place, usually next to the aft cabin bulkhead. Your plans should

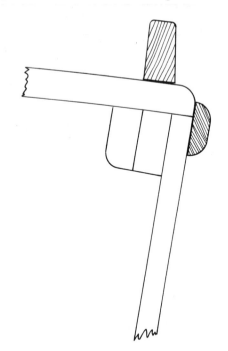

Figure 13-17B. Finished interior clamp with toerail and guard.

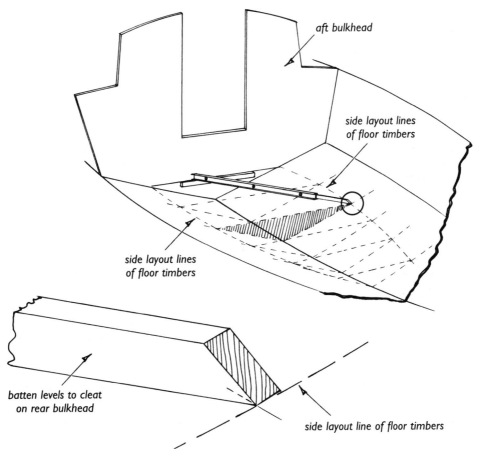

Figure 13-19. Laying out floor timbers using a level, marking along station layouts on the hull bottom.

state the depth of the floor timber at that point. If they don't, measure from the plans with an architectural scale rule. After marking the appropriate height on the bulkhead, use a small spirit level to mark a horizontal line on the bulkhead parallel with the athwartships waterline. Your floor timbers will probably have some uniform centerline-to-centerline spacing, most likely 16 to 24 inches on center or whatever your plans specify. Mark the centerline for each floor timber forward of the

aft bulkhead, and mark another set of layout points both port and starboard where each floor timber will lie. With a pencil, connect the layout marks.

Go back to your original horizontal marking along the aft cabin bulkhead and tack a small horizontal cleat on that line. With a long batten extension hold one end of the level on the cleat and mark an intersection with the edges of the floor timber layouts. Keep an eye on the level's bubble to pick off the ends of the floor timbers.

Cut several small battens the same width as the floor timbers and place them across the hull at the marks. Measure the depth of the "V" at the keel centerline, noting this dimension on a scrap of paper. Measure the beams (widths) and note them on your list. Draw in the floor timber widths and the centerline depths onto your pattern stock and cut out the patterns, and check for an accurate fit in the hull.

The floor timber templates may not fit precisely if you have already taped the seam in the keel of the boat. To compensate, set your pattern in place, level athwartships. With your pencil compass held exactly vertical and set at about ¼ inch, scribe the outline of the true bilge of the boat onto the pattern. Repeat this procedure for all of your patterns, and cut out along the scribed line. Your patterns will fit in place, but will be ¼-inch short of the true height. When you transfer the pattern to your floor timber stock, add ¼ inch to compensate for the extra height. I usually give these patterns ¼-inch or so extra height to allow me to scribe down into perfect position and height.

After cutting out the floor timbers, cut a limber hole in each one so that bilge water will be able to flow through and settle at the lowest point in the bilge. I prefer to put the limber holes to one side because most designs have keel bolts going through the centerline of the floor timbers. Cut the limber holes large enough to accommodate any anticipated bilge pump hoses and other plumbing that might run through the bilge.

Preseal the floor timbers with at least two coats of epoxy. When you install the timbers, bond them in place with ½-inch-deep wood flour fillets backed up with #14 x 1½-inch screws from outside the hull. I often roll another coat of epoxy over the whole bilge area—floor timbers, panels and all—after installation, just to ensure adequate protection from moisture.

For large boats with a lot of potential keel strain, I often sandwich dimensional floor timber stock between ½-inch marine plywood. Then I bond in these floor timbers with epoxy and glass seams to integrate them into the hull structure.

14

FILLETING AND GLASSING PLYWOOD JOINTS

Fillets (coved epoxy paste mixed with fillers) and fiberglass tape reinforcement are what make stitch-and-glue construction possible. Not only do epoxied joints weld the plywood panels together, but they effec- tively transfer structural loads from one sur- face to another to help avoid stress concen- trations—and this is truly the essence of what makes a sturdy, well-constructed stitch- and-glue boat such a strong and fine vessel.

Figure 14-1. This wood flour/epoxy filleting mixture has the right consis- tency to work well. Note the paddle-type stir stick used to spread the mix- ture into the joint.

After the plywood panels have been stitched or fastened into position, the joints and their adjacent surfaces must be coated first with unthickened epoxy. Coat the adjoining surfaces wider than your final seam width so that no point of the fillet-joint area will be epoxy-starved. For extra-strong, heavy-duty joints you can also distress the joint areas with a rough cross-grain grinding with a stiff phenolic grinding pad and a 36-grit paper. This cuts into the plywood veneers enough to give more effective keying across the joint area.

Once the joint areas have been coated, mix some wood flour and Cabosil into epoxy to create the filleting material. I use a mix of two-thirds wood flour to one-third Cabosil. The mixture should be thick: neither syrupy nor too stiff to work. To test for the proper consistency, hold the stirring stick vertically with a golfball-sized glob on the end of it; if any part of the mixture slides, it is still too thin. When the wood flour is too stiff, the mixture will appear a bit dry and will result in fillets peppered with hard-to-remove air holes. We are look-

Figure 14-2. This wood flour/epoxy mixture is almost too dry to apply properly. Note the holes left in the fillet after being squeegeed into the joint; they could lead to air holes in the laminated composite joint and compromise the strength of the joint. A bit more mixed epoxy added to the wood flour would correct the dryness.

ing for the consistency of a moderately stiff peanut butter.

Apply the thickened mixture to the joints using a plastic fillet squeegee custom-cut to shape on the job, smoothing over the lumps of filleting mixture. An alternative is to make a cone out of butcher paper, squeeze an even bead of fillet material into place, then squeegee the bead into a smooth, even, coved joint. This process is tidier but more time-consuming. Either way, you'll want to get the fillet mixture neatly into the joint and smoothed out to give the boat smooth, even joints.

The depth of the hull fillets should equal the thickness of the thickest piece of plywood being fastened, and should extend outward from the centerline of the joint 1½ to 2 times its thickness. Depending on the angle of the joint, the fillet might be wider. We want a smooth, curved transition from one panel to the next (see Figure 10-11).

With the fillets sculpted into shape, the next step is to apply the glass tape reinforcements. It is very important that the laminate be built up with the narrower cloth tapes placed over the fillets first, followed by incrementally wider layers. This allows the strength of the joint to gradually transit to the plywood panels—these tapered joints are much stronger and result in hull joints and seams that when stressed show a strength similar to the plywood panels they are bonding together.

Precut all of the runs of glass tape, carefully folding or draping each near the spot where it will be used. If your design uses multiple layers of glass tape, precut all the layers and arrange them into sets. Use masking tape to identify each set and its location. The more organized you are, the more professional the job will be in the end. Remember, once you mix epoxy you will have to work hard and fast; interruptions due to lack of preparation will only cost you money in lost epoxy, and will make a sticky job that much less enjoyable.

Work symmetrically in the boat when glassing the seams. For instance, tape the entire keel-and-stem joint in a small dinghy

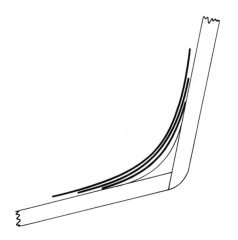

Figure 14-3. One method for overlapping fiberglass tape layers. . . .

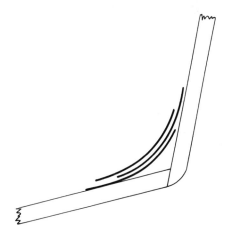

Figure 14-4. . . . and an alternative method with tapes of the same widths.

before starting on the chines. When you glass the chines, allow enough time, and have the materials ready, to do both chines in one session. It's easier if you keep your raw epoxy materials close at hand; you'll waste a lot of time and energy if you have to climb in and out of a large boat each time you need to mix a new batch of epoxy, and moving in and out of the hull also risks shifting the boat out of alignment during the critical bonding process.

I remember a small duck hunting boat we once built. After the hull seams were glassed, something about the boat seemed odd and out of place to me, though I couldn't immediately put my finger on it. A couple of days later, we discovered that the boat was ¾ inch out of square—it was twisted. That boat could never be fixed; no matter how many tries we made, the epoxy seams had permanently locked the twist into the boat. To this day, that boat is up in the rafters of my shop, a total waste of time and money. Moral: Check and double-check the squareness of your boat before you glass the seams. Measure carefully from stem to both transom corners to check for squareness and lack of twist.

Another trick to help stabilize the boat and stiffen it before a major glassing session is to tab all the seams with small fillets, essentially serving the same function as small weld tabs on a metalworking project. I tab the night before, at the least, so the epoxy fillets cure before I start going in and out of the boat a lot. You can run your regular fillet right over the tops of these tabs without a lot of bother.

I always fillet and glass the seams of my boats in one continuous session, without allowing the fillet or the individual layers of glass tape to cure. This obviates the need for sanding between layers to achieve a good secondary bond, and it is the most efficient way to build. Lay the fiberglass tape over the fillet joint and lightly smooth it into place with your gloved hand. Keep a sharp eye out for air bubbles, as they weaken the laminate. Consider getting a small, toothed fiberglass tooling roller to smooth out bubbles. Press the cloth in place, taking care not to dent excessively or shift the underlying soft fillet material. Brush additional unthickened epoxy over the fiberglass tape to complete the saturation. When the cloth is sufficiently saturated, its appearance will change from dry, silver-white to translucent. Air bubbles should be rolled or squeegeed out before

Figure 14-5. Close-up of epoxy tabs in place on hull joints, here a transom/bottom panel joint, before wire stitches have been removed, and before the major hull glassing of the interior seams.

Figure 14-6. A toothed roller aids in smoothing out the glass taping on interior hull joints and helps get rid of air bubbles.

Figure 14-7. A glassing box can make taping the interior seams a much easier job. It's imperative that all layers of this laminate be thoroughly wetted out before applying it to a seam.

the next layer of tape is applied. Repeat the process for each layer of fiberglass tape. Try to avoid applying additional epoxy as an overcoat to the final layer; it usually absorbs the excess epoxy from previous layers, creating a better resin-to-cloth ratio. After several minutes, if it is obvious that there are going to be some dry spots that won't saturate properly, carefully brush a bit of epoxy as needed to complete the saturation.

For first-class results that require much less sanding for a smooth seam, apply a layer of peel ply on top of your taped seams. Peel ply, a finely woven polyester cloth, is available from your epoxy or glass cloth supplier, and epoxy won't adhere well to it. Just press a strip of it down into the fresh joint, and allow the uncured epoxy of the joint to soak into it. Use a plastic squeegee to smooth the strip over the layers

Figure 14-8A. A glassing box allows the boat-builder to make final adjustments in the length of the seam laminates for more accurate fits.

of wet-out fiberglass tape, thus smoothing out and removing excess epoxy from the laminate. After the epoxy has cured, you simply peel off the strip, leaving a smooth joint surface. Peel ply is a wonderful time saver, almost completely eliminating the need to sand the surface once it is removed. Polyester dress lining, available from any fabric store, can work as a substitute for peel ply, but your best bet is to buy the real stuff.

Some small fillets that are not structural hull joints will not require fiberglass tape overlays. For these joints, mix the same wood flour fillet material and use the rounded end of a tongue depressor to cove the fillet surface. Let the fillet cure until it reaches the consistency of stiff modeling clay. At this point, use a piece of tightly woven cotton cloth—soaked in either lacquer thinner or isopropyl alco-

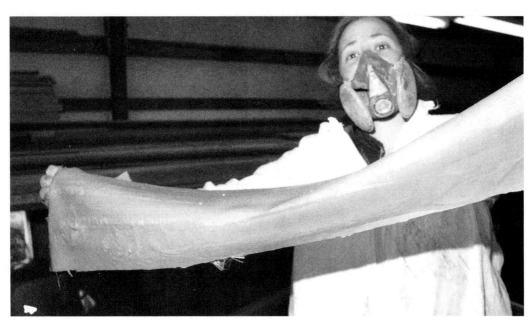

Figure 14-8B. A length of epoxy-saturated laminate ready to be placed on a seam. Note the worker's Tyvek suit and canister respirator. She should be wearing eye protection.

Figure 14-9. After the laminate has cured, the top (peel ply) layer can be pulled off and removed. Peel ply results in a much smoother laminate and shortens the sanding time.

hol—over the fingertip of a solvent-proof glove to smooth the surface. If you avoid denting or moving the semistiff fillet material, the surface will become so smooth that there will be little need for sanding later. In the case of a brightly finished (clear) surface, the cured, wood-colored fillets will blend with the natural wood color of the plywood panel.

Another way to save time and frustration when glassing joints is to make up a glassing box, which consists simply of a base of scrap plywood about 14 inches wide and about 6 to 8 feet long, to which are affixed sides and ends about 1 inch high. If you carefully measure and precut your fiberglass cloth strips for the joints, you can do a full wet layup of a glass joint away from the boat. In our shop, one worker mixes epoxy resin and fillet mater-

Figure 14-10. Wood flour fillets at the edges of the joints of fitted members will make joints stronger and more professional looking.

ial while another does cloth layups in the glass box and a third works in the hull under construction applying the fillets and the cloth strips.

The sequence goes like this: The person in the boat coats the plywood around the joints with unthickened epoxy provided by the person doing the mixing; he or she then is handed some freshly mixed filleting compound with which to cove the joints. Meanwhile the worker at the glassing box is laying up the fiberglass cloth portions of the hull seams in reverse order of application: first a wide layer of peel ply, then the widest layer of fiberglass cloth tape, then the next narrower, and finally the narrowest, saturating all the layers with epoxy resin. When all the air bubbles have been rolled or squeegeed out, the whole laminate is lifted out of the box and handed to the worker in the boat, who lays it over the fresh fillet material and rolls or squeegees out the last remaining air bubbles.

Working this way divides the labor into manageable chunks and minimizes confusion and mess. Try it with a couple of friends; your glassing day will go by quicker and more enjoyably. Don't forget appropriate refreshments at the end of the day to celebrate the completion of some good, hard work.

15

ROLLING OVER THE HULL

Once the major interior hull joints and bulkheads are glassed, the sheer reinforcement or clamps are in place, and the floor timbers installed, the hull must be rolled upside down to complete the exterior work. It's important that the interior structure is at a point where the hull can withstand the strains of rollover without damage. Remember though, that too much interior work will add weight and can make the rollover more difficult, increasing the chances of damage.

If you're working on a tight budget, a boom crane or other expensive machinery to assist the rollover is probably out of the question. You'll need to roll the hull the old-fashioned way: with manpower. How many willing helpers will it take? Here's a simple formula: Take the length of the boat, subtract 8, divide the remainder by 3, and round up to the nearest whole number for the optimal required manpower. For example, if your boat is 22 feet long: $(22-8)/3 = 4.75$. You'll need *at least* five people total to help you in the rollover. If you have mechanical aids such as jacks and stands, you might get by with fewer people. But there is another rule to keep in mind:

Your rolling party will take as much manpower as you have available. If you have five people you'll think you had just enough—if you have eight you'll think you could never have done the job with fewer.

You have two basic methods of rolling the boat over. You can roll as is without jigs or roller frames or you can fabricate a simple wooden rolling frame with which to hold the boat and cushion the rolling process. I have rolled boats up to 36 feet long without any jigs with little problem. But it is a bit easier on the nerves to have a rolling frame. It doesn't cost much more to build and can make for a much easier time.

Obviously, the area for the rollover must be clear of clutter and junk. Have sawhorses, jacks, and blocks ready. I keep some old tires, mattresses, cushions, and rolls of carpet handy to cushion the hull at its contact points with the floor during rollover.

Make sure that one person has been designated as the leader, and talk the rolling process through before you start. Who will do what, and in what sequence? You want to avoid finding yourself with sev-

Figure 15-1. A shop-made rollover jig can take a lot of stress out of the rollover process for a larger stitch-and-glue boat.

Figure 15-2A. Small and medium-sized boats can be rolled over with good guidance and the help of a lot of friends with strong backs. This 22-foot Surf Scoter powerboat will take the better part of an hour to roll over.

Figure 15-2B. Rolling the hull in stages, with breaks wherever you can block the hull and not worry about it falling.

Figure 15-2C. Once the hull is rightside up, it's fairly easy to hold upright until blocking or shoring can be put into place.

eral thousand pounds of weight and thousands of dollars of hull midway through the rollover, with conflicting opinions on what to do next!

During the lifting process, block the hull into position at intervals, and constantly check to make sure that no person is handling too much weight. When the gunwale is high in the air, with the hull's weight ready to pass the balance point and shift to the other side, move two or more people to the other side to catch and slow the hull as it rolls over. With the hull fully on its side, transfer people around to lower and block the hull in intervals, until the hull is in the full inverted position.

My shop is wood-framed, and the walls and ceiling cannot support the strains of tackles to lift or lower the hull. But I do occasionally use a block and tackle off the side walls to act as a safety brake, controlling the speed of rollover and assisting the rollover crew. With a 4:1 tackle and a scared, strong operator, the hull can be slowed down and safety assured; come-alongs work well for this also.

If your manpower stabilizes the hull at stem and stern, lifts and lowers in intervals, blocking for safety as you go, and constantly monitors where the weight is shifting, the rollover should go smoothly and safely, and a lot easier than you might suspect. But for hulls bigger than 35 feet you will definitely want a boom crane. For a couple of hundred dollars you can safely flip your labor of love and save a lot of grief.

The use of rolling jigs aids the rollover process but never entirely eliminates the basic job of lifting or jacking up the hull to the balance point then safely lowering it down on the other side. But if you think the process through and make sure you or your designated rolling leader has the last word and that all helpers know this, your rollover will go through without a hitch.

16

REMOVING WIRES

Wire stitches cannot be left in the hull because the normal heating and cooling cycles of the boat may cause the wires to migrate to the surface, marring the finish. I feel so strongly about this that at times we count the pulled wires to make sure every suture comes out.

In a small boat you can place runs of fillet material between the sutures, allow these to cure, then pull out the wires before glassing the joints inside and out. But in larger boats, where the hull is going to be walked in and the strains are greater, it may be better to complete all the interior hull seams with the full epoxy/fiberglass cloth composite joint, allow to cure, then remove the stitches. If you are an experienced builder and have full confidence in your hull, go ahead and tab your seams and pull out all stitches early before glassing interior seams. But it's not that big a deal to pull out stitches after the glassing has been done.

The wires used to stitch the panels together are only left in place until the filleted, taped seams have fully cured. Applying heat to the wires softens the cured epoxy enough to allow the stitches to be pulled with a pair of pliers. Some builders prefer to use a fast epoxy and remove the wires immediately, while the epoxy is still setting, but I like to wait overnight and remove the wires when the epoxy is more fully cured.

If you have cured epoxy seams over the wires, begin by untwisting the wire suture two or three turns, then clip the wire ends next to the twist so both ends can be easily grabbed with pliers. Apply heat, and when the end of the wire is glowing red-hot, allow a minute or so for the heat to transfer throughout the wire. Using your pliers, pull the wire toward you with a levering motion against a scrap wood block. The wire should ease out nicely. If the wire breaks inside the suture, simply heat the other end and pull that out.

There are two methods of heating the stitches. The first is to use a small hand-held propane torch, but in addition to the obvious fire hazard of using an open flame in your workshop, you must be sure to hold the torch parallel to the hull surface to avoid scorching the plywood.

In my shop, the preferred method utilizes a 12-volt battery and a set of jumper cables. Connect a jumper cable from the negative post of the battery to one of the wire ends, then connect a second jumper cable between the positive post and the carbon rod element from the center of a D-cell flashlight battery. (You will need to dissect a used battery to expose the post.) Hold the positive-post rod element briefly to the suture wire until it glows (the carbon rod helps eliminate the potential of arc welding the wire). Be careful not to connect the circuit too long, since it generates a lot of heat quickly. If you apply too much electricity the epoxy will flame or possibly burn the plywood panel. Experiment, and you will soon find how little contact time is needed to adequately heat the wires.

If I'm not using the battery method, I usually heat one or two wires ahead of myself and then return to the wires to pull them once the heat has transferred throughout the wire. Never leave pieces of wire in the hull. Dig the pieces out and fill in the hole with filleting material if need be.

Figure 16-1. A battery jig will heat the wire stitches to allow their removal from the hull. It's very important to remove the wires—they could work their way out of the joint over time.

Don't just plug the tops of the holes with filler; fill them with resin, which is fairly easy to do during the exterior sheathing process. (We'll discuss that later.)

17

COLD MOLDING THE
STITCH-AND-GLUE HULL

Larger stitch-and-glue boats might require a final skin thickness that limits the flexibility of the panels. A boat larger than 30 feet will require skins of ¾- to 1-inch thickness, but plywood that thick is hard to find and extremely difficult (read, impossible) to bend into shape. The solution is to use thinner, more flexible plywood for the initial stitch-up procedure to shape the hull. Then, once the interior joints are filleted and taped, some interior structure assembled, and the hull rolled over, layers of thin plywood can be laminated onto the hull exterior to build it up to the desired final thickness. I call this process "plywood cold molding," and have used it on hulls as short as 18 feet to achieve the correct shape and skin thickness, and as long as 48 feet to give them strength to stand up to their intended service duty.

This method of cold molding is easy and fast because you are using the initial stitch-and-glue hull as an integral mold, and it allows the stitch-and-glue builder access to larger boats that wouldn't be possible with single-layer skins.

If you have studied cold molding as it applies to round-bottomed boats, you learned to spile (shape) the planks to ensure full contact with the hull's surface. In stitch-and-glue construction, however, the hull is made entirely of developed plywood panels, so you can avoid spiling completely. The only shaping you need to do is rough-cutting your panels to easily place them on the boat.

I don't scarf the panels (or join end to end in a continuous sheet) when cold molding, and don't attempt to cold mold additional hull layers with any plywood thicker than ⅜ inch. The real cold-molding workhorse for me is ¼-inch plywood applied in single layers until the desired hull thickness is reached.

When you know that your hull will require cold molding to build up its final skin thickness, a good trick is to cut out the cold molded layers when you loft and cut the initial hull panels. Typically, I loft out my hull panels on my scarfed plywood sheets, then before cutting them I use the lofted patterns to lay out as many of the thinner cold-molding plywood panels as I'll need for the final laminate. While the initial stitch-and-glue panels need to be scarfed full length, these cold-molding

Figure 17-1. A 29-foot Means of Grace hull ready for the reinforcement provided by cold molding additional plywood layers.

layers can be simply butt joined—though its important to stagger the butt joints if several layers are to be applied. With this layering method it is quite simple to cut out the whole stack at one time, saving a lot of effort when the cold molding process begins.

The cold molding procedure is simple. Make sure you are well prepared, because once the epoxy is mixed it will begin setting up, and you must work fast. Take your precut panels for the first layer and place them in rough position on the boat. Staples or screws help hold the sheets in position until you have dry fitted the entire layer. Mark the position of each sheet carefully for its fit on the hull, indicating which face is up. After all the pan-

els have been fitted, remove the numbered sheets from the hull.

Next, drill ⅛- to 3/16-inch diameter holes about 6 to 8 inches on center throughout all the panels. These small holes help to prevent air entrapment between the layers. You can stack-drill these holes to help speed up the preparation process. Improbable though it seems, it is very common when you fasten a sheet of plywood around its perimeter, whether cold molding hull layers or laminating a deck, to trap large bubbles of air between the layers. The small holes allow air to escape, and you will know you have good contact between layers when you see a small amount of epoxy resin ooze out of each hole. The epoxy oozes will also act like nails to help bond the two layers together.

Mix the epoxy *without thickeners* and roll a generous amount on the face-down sides of the panels to be cold molded. Set these aside while rolling an equally generous coat on the hull of the boat. If you notice gouges or holes in the hull or the panels, fill them with thickened epoxy. Make sure every surface and edge of the hull and the cold-molding stock is coated with epoxy before positioning and fastening the plywood to the hull.

I usually use pneumatic, air-powered staplers with stainless steel or Monel bronze wire staples in a variety of sizes and lengths to fasten the layers to the hull. If you don't own a power stapler, consider

renting one. Hand staplers, bronze ring-shank boat nails, and small screws will also work. Place a fastener at least every 4 to 6 inches to guarantee contact between pieces until the epoxy cures. You should have a good ooze out of the small holes; trapped air produces a hollow sound when you run your hand over the panels, and it's a good idea to check out the whole surface to make sure no air is trapped.

Some designs have so much shape in portions of the boat that even ¼-inch plywood in large sheets won't take the bend easily. In these cases, cut 4-inch-wide strips from the ¼-inch plywood and apply these diagonally to the hull just as you would the larger sheets. Make sure that you coat the

Figure 17-2. Cold molding the bottom bow sections of this 29-foot Black Crown powerboat is best accomplished by using smaller 4- to 6-inch-wide strips of plywood applied diagonally. Note the use of epoxy and fillers in gaps to eliminate any air voids or entrapment.

strips with epoxy. Don't spare the fasteners, and work fast and organized.

After the epoxy has cured, prepare the final exterior surface for fiberglass sheathing. Pull the mechanical fasteners within 4 inches of the chines, stem, keel, and other edges since those areas must be radiused before fiberglass can be applied, and the edge tools used for the radiusing would quickly dull if they came into contact with fasteners. Also check for fasteners standing proud of the surface; either set (drive below the surface) or pull these. I use a large screwdriver and mallet to set staples. Grinding fasteners off is an invitation to trouble, since the buried remnants could

eventually migrate through the fiberglass just as wire stitches will if not pulled. It would be best in a perfect world to pull out all fasteners, but that rarely is possible.

Cold mold as many layers of thin plywood onto the hull as needed to attain designed thickness—even more if desirable to compensate for rough usage such as ice or deadheads or prolonged dry storage on a trailer. Additional layers in a localized area of the hull or deck may be necessary to dissipate such stresses and strains as a side-mounted winch for oceanographic work or commercial fishing. A little extra protection is pretty easy to add now, but a lot harder later on.

18

KEELS, RUDDERS, SKEGS, AND OTHER APPENDAGES

Rudders, centerboards, skegs, keels, stem bands, and other appendages can be pre-built from dimensional wood or laminated plywood stock. Since keels and skegs are potentially high wear or heavily loaded structures, take great care in securing them to the hull and protecting them from moisture penetration. I use bolts and screws in addition to bedding them in epoxy to assure proper attachment, and also use adequate filleting and glass tape reinforcements to keep the appendage from being wrenched out of position if stressed. On the bottom or outermost surface of a keel and stem band, I prefer to use ironbark—a durable hardwood—as a shoe for a more durable, replaceable chafing surface. But a lot of people prefer a stainless steel or brass half oval band to help with chafing. Either method works fine and is a worthwhile addition to the boat.

Sheathe the interior of the center-board or daggerboard trunk with the same considerations as the exterior of the hull. And it's important that all plywood surfaces be fully sealed before the sheathing is applied, since these areas would be almost impossible to service later. Another alter-native in the inside of a centerboard case is to forgo fiberglass sheathing. I sometimes protect the interior surfaces with a layer of 1/16-inch countertop laminate glued with epoxy resin to the plywood, thus providing a slick and durable shield against the board's friction and loading pressures. This eliminates the need for additional fiberglass sheathing and makes for quite a durable installation.

When using the countertop laminate, stop a couple of inches from the bottom of the trunk, leaving a sufficient landing for the hull's cloth sheathing to wrap around the edges. This also facilitates fairing. Glue the laminate in place with epoxy before assembling the case.

Assemble the case or trunk as a stand-alone structure and insert it so as to protrude several inches beyond the hull surface, using heavy fillets and glass cloth laminates to secure it inside the hull. After these fillets have cured, trim the excess flush with the hull. When you later sheathe the exterior (Chapter 19), overlap at least 1½ inches of cloth up into the interior of the case or trunk. The edge of the dagger-board case or centerboard trunk is

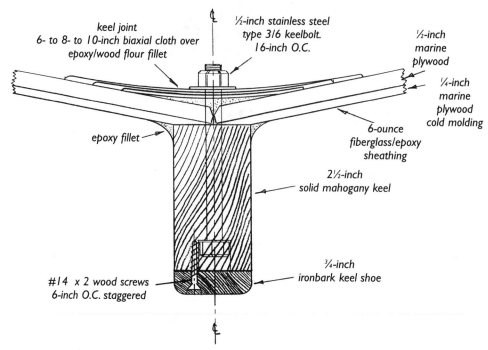

keel joint
6- to 8- to 10-inch biaxial cloth over
epoxy/wood flour fillet

½-inch stainless steel
type 3/6 keelbolt.
16-inch O.C.

½-inch
marine
plywood

¼-inch
marine
plywood
cold molding

epoxy fillet

6-ounce
fiberglass/epoxy
sheathing

2½-inch
solid mahogany keel

#14 x 2 wood screws
6-inch O.C. staggered

¾-inch
ironbark keel shoe

Figure 18-1. Typical 30-foot hull bottom/keel stitch-and-glue joint.

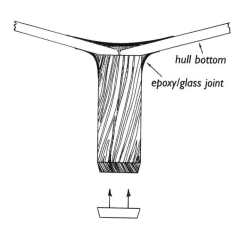

hull bottom

epoxy/glass joint

Figure 18-2. Ironbark worm shoe.

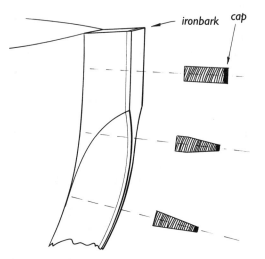

ironbark   cap

Figure 18-3. Stem with ironbark cap, and its cross section at various heights.

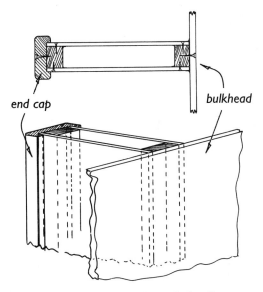

end cap

bulkhead

Figure 18-4. Daggerboard trunk details.

extremely vulnerable, and it's important to use enough cloth to strengthen this area of the hull.

All these structures must be carefully sheathed in fiberglass cloth and epoxy (see Chapter 19), and whether it's best to apply them before or after your exterior hull sheathing will vary with the particular design you are building and with your building schedule. Certain appendages such as a centerboard trunk or a daggerboard trunk are best built up and installed in the boat before the hull's exterior sheathing. But the exterior stem and keel on a boat like Surf Scoter are best applied after the exterior hull sheathing is completed and then glassed in place separately.

19

Sheathing the Exterior

A durable outer skin of fiberglass cloth set in epoxy adds a great deal of strength and abrasion resistance to a stitch-and-glue boat. Unsheathed and exposed plywood is much more vulnerable to abrasion or impact damage, which could lead to moisture penetration. Sheathing also assures a thick, consistent epoxy matrix over the entire surface of the structure, and spreads the stresses of use over its tough coat. Moreover, the maintenance of boats sheathed with cloth and epoxy is greatly reduced, coming much closer to that theoretical ideal, the fiberglass boat. I use either 4- or 6- or 8-ounce fiberglass cloth, depending on the intended service. The 4-ounce cloth will result in a smoother final surface since the thicker yarn bundles of the 6-ounce or 8-ounce cloth tend to print-through (show a cloth pattern in the final painted surface over time), so I use the 4-ounce cloth on yachts that are to be finished with a dark paint. For workboats and other craft anticipating rougher duty, or boats to be painted a cooler, lighter color, 6- or 8-ounce cloth works best.

The cloth can be applied either wet or dry. The wet method calls for coating the hull with epoxy before laying the cloth. In the dry method, the cloth is draped over the hull surface, then epoxy is applied to the cloth. I prefer the dry method because the cloth is much easier to manage, and it makes a sticky job much more manageable.

There are other cloths that can be used for sheathing, mainly Dynel, Xynole/polyester, Kevlar, or polypropylene. While I have no particular gripe with using any of these cloths, I have no evidence that would prompt me to switch from glass cloth. The synthetics can be quite a bit harder to handle and work with than glass cloth, they are expensive, and your sources of supply are much more limited.

Application techniques for glass and synthetics can be approached in approximately the same manner. Synthetic cloths such as Dynel and Xynole/polyester come in lightweight 4-ounce and 4.3 ounce weights, respectively, but they tend to bulk up to the equivalent thickness of approximately 8-ounce glass cloth when wetted out with epoxy.

APPLYING CLOTH WITH
THE DRY METHOD

First, with 80-grit sandpaper sand the wooden hull surfaces to be sheathed to provide a mechanical tooth for the epoxy. I prefer the wider 50-inch fiberglass cloth to 38-inch cloth because it more easily covers the panels. Precut to length the pieces (panels) of cloth so you won't have to make cuts later with sticky hands. And it's a good idea to add about 10 percent to the length to allow working room. When laying out the cloth sections, try to keep the topsides sheathing joints low or below the waterline. Make sure all hull edges have been faired and smoothed or rounded over, so the cloth will lie smooth and flat over the plywood.

Coat all exposed plywood edges with unthickened epoxy, thoroughly saturating the edges to seal them completely with several coats. Although this can be done just prior to draping the cloth panels on the hull, it's easier if you coat the edges a day or two earlier and lightly sand the cured epoxy before finally positioning the cloth for sheathing.

It's easiest to work with a partner when sheathing. With your partner, grab each end of the cloth panel, pulling gently to keep it off the floor and suspended just over the hull. Now drop the dry cloth in position, smoothing out wrinkles with your hands; you'll see it has a natural tendency to smooth out. Then mix and pour small quantities of unthickened epoxy on the uppermost parts of the cloth panel. With a plastic squeegee, move the epoxy until it uniformly saturates the cloth, using a figure-eight motion to hold the resin on

Figure 19-1. Glass cloth sheathing laid out on the cabin top of a 29-foot Black Crown powerboat. This step allows the boatbuilder to trim accurately and keep the job as neat as possible.

the cloth. Begin in the middle of the piece and work toward the bow and stern; that way the minor stretch of the fiberglass panel has somewhere to go. Leave at least a 4-inch overlap on each of the cloth panels, wetting out only one panel at a time. I overlap at the chines, stems, and transom edges, making sure at least two layers of cloth are on every joint or seam to ensure extra strength.

If your pieces do not overlap on the chines and other joints, use an additional layer of cut fiberglass cloth tape there. In boats expecting rugged service, you might want three layers of cloth over all joints. Again, try to keep the mass of the overlaps below the waterline to minimize the amount of fairing you'll have to do on the visible portions of the hull; you won't always succeed, but try anyway.

Make sure that all of the fabric has been completely saturated with epoxy, but

Figure 19-2. Trimmed and smoothed, the cloth is wetted out. Mix up large buckets of epoxy, pour over the glass, and with a squeegee, use a figure-eight motion to saturate the cloth and the plywood below. Note the Tyvek gauntlets to protect the worker's forearms.

don't leave too much epoxy on the cloth, because the cloth can have a tendency to float around. After saturating the cloth, squeegee out excess epoxy. The cloth surface should have a clear, dull appearance, and the weave of the cloth will still be quite visible and show a cloth texture. If you wait a couple of hours you can come back and roll another layer of unthickened epoxy over the now-sheathed hull. But if you have to wait overnight, sand lightly before recoating.

After the epoxy has cured, use a grinder with an 8-inch pad and 80-grit discs to lightly sand the rough edges of the cloth overlaps. Hand-sand the true edges of the chines and other edges to avoid cutting into or damaging the cloth. Fair and smooth the surface in preparation for a second coating of unthickened epoxy, which must be rolled on evenly. This coat should completely fill the weave of the cloth; if not, a third coat should be applied, wet on wet over the second coat. If you have waited overnight or longer before applying the second coat to the sheathing, wash the area with clean water then dry it off. Your sandpaper will not gum up quite as fast and you will avoid contaminating the epoxy and glass cloth surface.

To avoid a rough, dimpled epoxy surface (roller stipple pattern), use a heat gun

Figure 19-3. Overlapping the glass cloth joints provides strength and ensures the integrity of the hull's exterior. The taped-off area of the transom will be finished bright.

to warm the epoxy so it flows out and smooths itself. After heating the surface, I often brush the epoxy lightly with one of the 4-inch foam throwaway brushes or with a split foam roller to smooth the surface.

20

Sanding and Fairing

Stitch-and-glue boatbuilding requires a considerable amount of sanding and fairing, although much of the interior hull seams and bulkhead sanding can be avoided by using peel ply on the taped composite seams. You must take considerable care to never cut into the layers of fiberglass cloth when you sand; use the sanding surface as a guide: The epoxy/cloth laminate is fairly translucent and when sanded creates white dust, but when you sand into the cloth, the surface will become silvery. Use the color variance as a guide to how deeply you are sanding.

Try to work only one area of the disc's surface when using a disc sander. Lift one edge of the disc slightly to help keep it cool, controlling the contact area to one position in relation to the disc. The greater the friction and heat, the faster the sanding disc will dull. Using light pressure also keeps the sander from walking

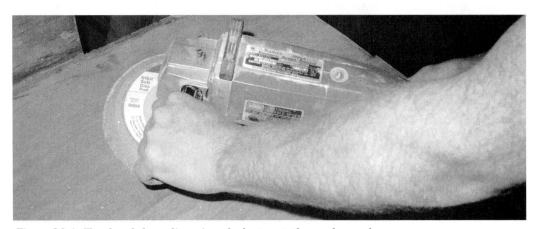

Figure 20-1. Two-handed sanding gives the best control over the sander. When the rear of the sander is lifted slightly, the sandpaper will throw off dust and run cooler.

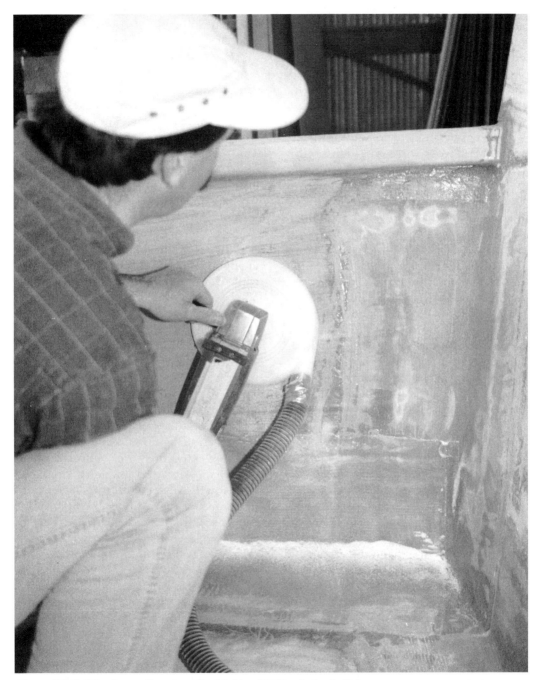

Figure 20-2. The dust collector on the Makita 9207 grinder/polisher makes the nasty job of sanding much more pleasant.

around and getting out of control. On the hull exterior, never sand corners, tight edges, stems, chine or keel lines, or transom edges with the disc sander; the epoxied cloth edges can be quickly sanded through, even by the most skilled operator. Confine the disc sander to open, flat surfaces, sanding corners or joints by hand. Most work with an 8-inch sander-polisher employs 80-grit discs.

Use epoxy to recoat spots where the cloth weave has been exposed by sanding. Keep in mind that different epoxy fillers sand with varying degrees of ease, depending on the density of the mixture. Wood flour is relatively difficult to sand, something to bear in mind when you are using that mixture to fill imperfections.

Use microballoons mixed with epoxy for repairs you need to sand out smoothly and easily. Use an epoxy/microballoon mixture to help even out glass cloth overlaps and any air bubbles that show up in the sheathing. If not filled, airholes will cause grief in the final finish.

One trick when repairing gouges is to use cellophane packing tape, sometimes called gator tape, to hold the epoxy filler material in the repair area, preventing the mixture from sagging out of place while curing. The tape acts as a sort of poor man's peel ply and maintains a smooth surface that requires less final sanding after the patch cures. Sand the repair spot smooth and recoat the surface with unthickened epoxy.

After fairing the hull and before painting, apply a final coat of epoxy. This last step thoroughly and uniformly seals the entire structure, provides additional moisture-proofing, and creates a smooth, stable base for the paint. Lightly sand this last coat with 220-grit sandpaper on a random orbit sander or a small palm sander.

Many of these sanding tools are now available with dust collection systems to aid in removal of sanding dust. You can stay a lot more comfortable and make the sanding job a lot more pleasant if you attempt to eliminate a lot of the dust. Fein Power Tools Company of Pittsburgh makes the best state-of-the-art dust removal system and tools compatible with that system. If you can afford it, these make fine companions during those many sanding hours.

Also don't neglect wearing a respirator, and by all means don't go skimpy on changing out your sandpaper frequently—while dull sandpaper can still cut, it takes a lot more pressure and is harder on the sanding tools and the sander than it needs to be. Changing sandpaper frequently helps keep you and the job efficient.

Don't forget to wash off the greasy by-products of the epoxy curing process with clean water and dry the surface before starting your sanding. This cleaning of the surface will allow your sandpaper to cut cleanly and clog up much less than if you had neglected this step. Simply wipe off with clean water and towel dry with clean shop towels. Washing off the surfaces also helps ensure that you don't contaminate the epoxied surface. (And speaking of shop towels, check with a local diaper service. Most will sell somewhat tattered but clean diapers for not too steep a price.)

While most epoxy companies advertise that recoating without sanding is possible up to 72 hours after the first coat is applied, I feel it's best to sand between any epoxy coats that have sat more than 24 hours. In most cases I sand even if it's only been overnight.

21

MARKING THE WATERLINE
AND PAINTING THE BOTTOM

MARKING THE WATERLINE

The smart move is to paint your boat's bottom before turning the hull rightside up. Before painting, you must locate and mark the waterline, which is much easier to do while the hull is still upside-down. Begin by leveling the inverted boat fore-and-aft and athwartships. From your plans, determine the freeboard from the waterline to the top of the sheer at the stem and at the two transom corners (just as we did originally to true the hull). Measure from the floor (assuming that it's reasonably flat) up to the stem and add that dimension to the freeboard to determine the waterline point. I usually don't mask to the designed waterline, but allow the boat's antifouling bottom coating to extend anything from an inch to a couple of inches above the designed flotation waterline, depending on the size of the boat. This allows for an antifouling splash zone and guards against the possibility of grass growing right at the waterline, and allows for slight

variation in weight of your finished boat.

Measure up from the floor and mark the hull stem at that point of intersection, then do same for the corners of the transom. If your shop floor is quite level you can mock up a simple marking jig with a sawhorse and some sticks. Move around the inverted hull, marking as many waterline points as you need.

If your shop floor is not level, use a water level or a transit. Clamp a length of clear hose between the stem and transom corners, with a bight of hose hanging down between those points. Fill the hose with water until the ends of the water column are at the boat's waterline, then move one end of the hose along the hull to mark the waterline fore and aft. The more marks you make, the easier it will be to mask the line.

The next step is to stretch masking tape along the marks. Pull long stretches of tape with even pressure, progressing from stem to transom. Keep the tape parallel to the markings as you apply it. Lightly press the tape into place; do not rub it firmly until the whole side of the hull has been masked. When you go back to do this, sight along the hull with your eyes at waterline height. If the masking line appears crooked, sight it from as far away as possible to double check. If there is a crooked section, do not rip off the tape, but use it as a reference for a second line of tape applied over the first.

BOTTOM PAINTING

Depending on where you will use your boat, the best bottom coating will be an antifouling paint. There are several antifoulants to choose from, including antifouling paints and epoxy-copper antifouling coatings. Paints are generally oil-based, although there is a trend toward water-based formulas to conform to new environmental regulations. I have found that you can paint any of these over a sanded epoxy coated bottom (220 grit) with good results. The problem with antifouling paints is that they must be renewed annually. They are soft and don't wear well, particularly on a trailered boat that is in and out of the water a great deal. Antifouling paints are expensive, too, so there is a substantial investment in annual recoating material and labor costs.

Epoxy-copper antifouling coatings are very expensive, but help avoid yearly application. These coatings are finely ground copper, copper/nickel, or copper-oxide within an epoxy resin base. They must be mixed with an epoxy system and can be applied to the bottom with a roller or sprayer. The copper is toxic to marine animal life and wards off marine plant growth, so the only yearly maintenance is lightly wet-sanding the bottom to expose fresh, nonoxidized copper particles. Manufacturers recommend about 20 mils (.02 inch) of coating thickness to ensure sufficient coverage. Since .75 to 1.0 mil will erode each

year, the life expectancy of the coating (according to the manufacturers) is 10 to 15 years. This is optimistic, but even if the lifetime is half that, the coating is still economical. Another benefit is that if you take the time to carefully sand, smooth, and buff the bottom of the hull after application you can achieve a slick, almost friction-free surface, which creates a much faster sailboat or more efficient powerboat. I believe these coatings are the closest to being environmentally responsible, and in the long run they can save the boatowner a considerable amount of money. On my boats they are becoming a common bottom-coating application. They can also function as a good base for conventional antifouling paints, providing longer-term protection for explorations into areas where annual haulouts might be difficult or impossible.

Avoid using marine enamel paint for bottom coatings. Topside enamels are not designed to withstand constant immersion, and they blister and fail rapidly under water. Only for the smallest skiff or dinghy would I consider applying a topsides paint to underwater surfaces.

Prepare the faired, smooth hull with a final sanding with 220-grit sandpaper, sanding the corners by hand. Dust the freshly sanded surface and clean areas of suspected contamination with water. Apply antifouling paint directly on the dry, sanded hull, over an epoxy primer. I use a product called Ditzler DP 40, which adheres well to the epoxied hull and provides a good base for bottom paints. (Actually DP 40 works well as a conversion coat for all paints.)

If you use an epoxy-copper antifouling system, roll the coating thickly over the freshly sanded hull bottom, and use disposable foam brushes to tip it off. It takes

Figure 21-1. Bottom coating in process on a 22-foot Surf Scoter powerboat with inboard diesel engines. The shaft tube has not yet been trimmed. Note the dishes on each side of the stern tube for better water access to the propeller.

a bit of finesse to get the application both thick and smooth, and it may take two or three coats to build up the necessary 20-mil thickness. This epoxy antifoulant is slow-curing, and may require several days between applications: don't hurry the process. Between coats, use 220-grit sandpaper to smooth the surface and impart a bit of tooth for the next coating.

22

RIGHTING THE HULL

We've already rolled the hull once; the procedure is fundamentally the same this time around, except that you must be careful not to damage the sheathing or exterior appendages or mar the soon-to-be painted topside surfaces. Take extra precautions to pad the floor and clear the area of anything that might damage the hull.

This rollover is always a heady time, mixing anxiety with enthusiasm. You will experience one of the finer moments of boatbuilding when you first see the true waterline as the hull is positioned rightside up. Take a moment to appreciate how much has been accomplished, and imagine the finished boat. Try to keep your rollover slow and well-organized, and don't let your enthusiasm get the best of you. There's still a lot of work ahead, but you've gone a long way toward breathing life into a pile of materials.

Figure 22-1. This 29-foot Means of Grace has just been rolled rightside up and is ready for interior finishing and launching.

23

INTERIOR STRUCTURES

Once you have savored the exuberance of completing the hull, it's time for a dose of reality. Climb into the boat with an armload of plans, a framing square, tape measure, felt-tipped pen, and a couple of long, stiff battens.

Your hull, now rightside up, should be leveled to the waterline both fore-and-aft and athwartships. Keep in mind that each step of the remaining construction needs to happen in its given order and with sufficient time and effort. Don't be overwhelmed by the number of projects yet to be completed, and resist making a list of them. Just pick them off one by one. Guard against post-rollover stall-out. When I was younger, I enjoyed long-distance running, which any runner will tell you involves mind over matter. Strength and stamina are secondary to mental resolve, and the key is to stay focused and not be distracted by the distance that remains. Find your rhythm, keep a steady pace, and go one step at a time.

MAST STEP

If the boat you are building is a sailboat, you must construct the mast step (if you did not do so earlier, before turning the boat upside down for sheathing), a structure that bears the weight of the mast and withstands the compression loading and strain of the mast heel. If your design calls for a deck-stepped mast, you'll need to build a structure from the deck to the keel to distribute the compression loads. Generally, the mast step can be viewed as an extension of the floor timber/cabin sole gridwork. It may be as simple as an

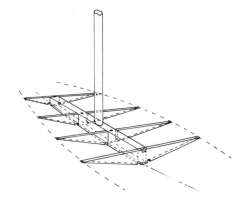

Figure 23-1. Look at the mast step as an extension of the floor timber/cabin sole gridwork, though in a larger boat the load must be spread over a greater area.

extra longitudinal spanning two floor timbers, though in a larger boat, the load must be spread over a greater area. The compression forces from a mast are considerable, so build sufficient strength into the mast step and seal it against moisture invasion. If your mast is keel-stepped and the base of the mast tenons into the mast step, provide a drain hole from the bottom of the mortise into the bilge. No matter what kind of mast boot you put at the partners, some moisture will still run down the mast and into the mortise.

CABIN SOLES

Assuming your floor timbers are glued in the bilge of the boat, lay out the floor timber lengths and distances on center (see Chapter 13) on ½- or ¾-inch plywood stock, and mark the athwartships centerline and half-widths of each floor timber measurement. The resultant layout represents your cabin sole, marked upside down on the cabin sole stock. With a flexible batten, fair the two curved edges. The next step is to provide bilge access through the center of the sole. I like to have continuous access, 6 to 8 inches wide for the entire length of the sole as in Figure 23-2. Use a polyurethane adhesive to fasten epoxy-sealed cabin soles to the floor timbers; adhesive caulking is less messy than epoxy and has good gap-filling capability. Place two beads on top of each floor timber and gently lay the cabin sole over the floor timber grid. Place at least four fasteners per floor timber, evenly spaced. Provide ventilation to the bilge by drilling several holes in the bilge access plate. Screwing the sole piece onto the floor timbers and glassing the edges onto the hull creates an extremely strong floor timber/cabin sole gridwork.

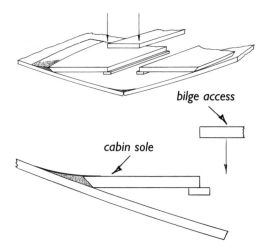

Figure 23-2. Bilge access through cabin sole showing glassing at edges.

COCKPIT SOLES

Cockpit soles differ from cabin soles in that the cockpit sole almost always attaches to cleats fastened to the bulkheads and hull sides for the simple reason that it's usually much higher in the boat. The cockpit soles must be carefully bonded to the structures surrounding them so that they are watertight, and water must be able to run off cleanly without puddling. My Nancy's China design presented a dicey problem in that the daggerboard trunk starts just forward of the rear bulkhead, and forward of the daggerboard trunk the bilge contains 385 pounds of ballast, nearly filling the entire space. It would be quite difficult to limber through the rear bulkhead and alongside the daggerboard trunk, and the bilge is inaccessible and extremely hard to drain, ventilate, and monitor for integrity. The solution was to fill the bilge below the cockpit sole with two-part polyurethane foam and bond the epoxy-sealed sole in place with no openings through the top. A separate bilge compartment and access forward of the daggerboard trunk allows the ballast to be cast in place and helps to ventilate that compartment. In general, if you can't adequately limber and ventilate, fill completely with two-part polyurethane foam and bond it solidly to the overlying piece. All parts must be scrupulously epoxy sealed before bonding.

LONGITUDINAL BULKHEADS

The longitudinal bulkheads form part of the framing structure of larger stitch-and-glue designs, particularly those with decks. These are nothing more than large bulkheads turned lengthwise in the boat.

The Surf Scoter cockpit has two longitudinal bulkheads running from the transom to the rear of the pilothouse bulkhead. These form the sides of the outboard motor well, the sides of the fuel tank compartment, and the adjoining side supports for the stern seats, and they provide bearing and fastening for the cockpit sole. The thrust of the outboard is dispersed throughout the boat's structure by these two cockpit longitudinals. All longitudinals are bonded into place with taped seam fillet joints with the same care as in the major athwartships bulkheads.

Figure 23-3. Cabin sole and floor timbers in the 29-foot Means of Grace. Note that the cabin sole is glassed into the hull bottom at its edges, effectively tying into the hull the floor timber grid and the ballast keel that will eventually hang from that grid.

Figure 23-4. The 22-foot Surf Scoter's cockpit showing the integration of both athwartships bulkheads and the two longitudinal bulkheads. The latter bulkheads support the outboard in its motorwell and define the cockpit floor height. The fuel tank stows between the longitudinals.

BERTH FLATS

Berth flats are like large, horizontal bulkheads. In most stitch-and-glue boats, they are positioned between major athwartships bulkheads. Their outboard edges usually contact the hull, while their inboard edges terminate atop a longitudinal berth bulkhead. The berth flat, if it is fastened to the hull and to athwartships and longitudinal bulkheads, can add a great deal of strength to the boat. It helps to transfer strains in the boat's structure to other strong points in the hull.

Berth flats can be built of ½- or ¾-inch plywood. If the flat is also functioning as a settee in the main part of the cabin, opt for the heavier stock. If the berth flat is in a forward V-berth area in a small boat that will be used only for sleeping, ½-inch plywood will be more than adequate.

The berth flat should be bonded to the surrounding structures with epoxy fillets and taped joints to make it an integral part of the overall boat's structure. You can gain access for stowage and ventilation through the longitudinal bulkhead with pigeon holes or doors, or through rectangular cutouts in the flat. Be sure to provide adequate ventilation.

FIDDLES

Fiddles retain things that are stowed on shelves or flats, be they cushions, books,

Figure 23-5. The floor grid of a Means of Grace, showing the berth longitudinal faces installed and bonded onto the cabin sole. The next step will be bonding the berth flats onto this structure, and bonding the outboard edge of the flat to the hull sides. Note the cleats at the outboard edges of the hull to support the berth flats.

or pots and pans—they also trim, finish, and accent a boat's interior.

I use dark hardwood for fiddles, and I don't usually epoxy-seal or varnish them because over time they get scratched and gouged when the boat is used. If you use a blond-colored wood, deep scratches will generally stain dark and become very noticeable. Finish and protect the wood with several coats of Deks Olje, Seafin, or a similar oil. A few days after applying the last coat of oil, I apply a coat of Trewax furniture wax and buff the pieces. This finish looks a lot like hand-rubbed varnish but can be easily touched up with more wax. An annual waxing keeps the fiddles looking soft, smooth, and ship-shape. And by using darker mahogany-type hardwoods,

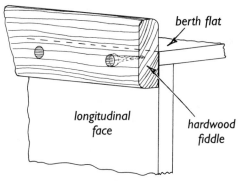

Figure 23-6. Bungs should run parallel to the grain of fiddles.

the inevitable gouges and scratches won't be as noticeable as they might in a light-colored wood.

I attach the fiddles with countersunk

145

holes and stainless steel sheet metal screws, 8 to 12 inches apart. Glue the wood bungs with a quick-setting epoxy or a cyanoacrylate adhesive (instant glue) of the gap-filler type, and make sure that the grain in the wood bungs parallels the grain in the fiddle. Cut the bungs out of rippings or end cuts from the fiddle stock to match the surrounding wood color. Running the bungs with the grain parallel to the grain of the fiddles looks less distracting to the eye the running it at 90 degrees to the grain.

ACCESS AND VENTILATION

The ability to access every section and compartment of the boat is important for inspection, maintenance, and in the event of hull damage. Complete access also helps in another critical area: ventilation. As a basic rule, you can never have too much ventilation in a boat. The marine environment is extreme and can run from either cool and moist to hot and humid, and either way you are dealing with a lot of moisture. Provide multiple openings for ventilation, especially if the openings are smaller than 12 square inches. For truly efficient ventilation, the access holes should be in the ends of the compartment to establish an air flow pattern, providing fresh air at one end and flushing stale air at the other, a breathing effect of sorts.

I use several methods to provide adequate ventilation and access. In vertical bulkheads, I cut large openings called pigeon holes. The doorless pigeon holes not only provide good ventilation and access, but organize gear efficiently. Doors require ventilation slots with small bronze, stainless steel, or wood covers. Cut from ¼-inch plywood, wood covers can be gang-

Figure 23-7. A completed Means of Grace berth flat. Note the glassing at the outboard edge; the access liftout exposes the smooth epoxy-sealed interior. All components of the hull must be finished to this extent.

produced on a drill press with a sharp, brad-point drill and screwed over a hole cut into the door or bulkhead. Occasionally, I cut out my bird-shaped logo, particularly if the boat has a painted interior. You can make all sorts of decorative patterns; use your imagination.

For storage access to the berth and sole flats, use a rectangular cutout in the plywood with a couple of 1½-inch-diameter fingerholes. Bolt a couple of wood cleats on at least two sides of the flat to support the cutout lid. Latches are unnecessary, since gravity and the weight of the cushions keeps the cutout in place. (On an offshore boat, however, I'd latch down the cutouts.)

Every cabin should have at least two sources of fresh air. In a boat as small as our 15-foot Nancy's China, they might include one cowl-type ventilator at the bow (which can also be used as a chainfall for the anchor rode) and a series of vent holes drilled in the companionway drop slides. A larger boat like the Surf Scoter might want two cowl vents on the pilothouse roof and one cowl vent in the forward hatch. Two solar-powered ventilators would be even better; use one as an intake on the forward hatch and the second as an exhaust vent in the pilothouse roof.

Don't skimp on the ventilation system for your boat; provide for worst-case scenarios under different weather and wind conditions. And remember, a boat is very much like a house: A lived in and used house keeps a lot better than one that is closed up and stale for long periods.

HATCHES

There is a wide variety of hatch designs to choose from. I use two basic types, both of which are easily made. An ideal choice for the waters of the Pacific Northwest is a hardwood box with finger-jointed or dovetailed corner joints, fitted with a translucent Lexan (polycarbonate) or solid wood top.

If you choose a Lexan top, overbore pilot holes in the Lexan at least one drill size larger than the fastener diameter. Polycarbonate expands and contracts with temperature changes and overboring the pilot holes allows the Lexan to move without cracking around the fasteners. Bed the Lexan in a polyurethane bedding compound. Applying a clear primer to the Lexan will help the caulking compound adhere to it. Set the screws with hand pressure evenly around the hatch frame. Fasteners every 3 inches is the minimum for bedding ¼-inch Lexan; ⅜-inch Lexan requires a fastener every 4 inches. If you don't like the look of the Lexan edge, trim it with a half-round of hardwood. If the

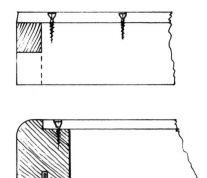

Figure 23-8. Hatch section types.

clear hatch does not ensure sufficient privacy, light sanding with 220-grit sandpaper followed by a scuffing with Scotchbrite pads will frost it, while still allowing plenty of light below.

For the solid-wood top, build the frame first and rout the perimeter with a rabbet bit. Set the hatch frame upside down over a piece of ½- or ¾-inch plywood stock and mark the outline of the frame. Cut along the outline, carefully dry fit the piece, and epoxy the top into place.

I like to make a hatch cover more attractive by cutting a series of small grooves in the hatch with a table saw and a kerf or dado blade. Gluing a piece of contrasting wood into the grooves creates an inlaid hatch with the watertight integrity of solid plywood. Carefully seal the hatch with epoxy and apply a minimum of six coats of varnish.

Figure 23-9. A curved hatch with glued inlays.

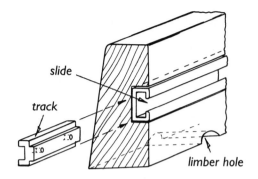

Figure 23-10. Taco Metals extrusion hatch slides.

With minor variations, the same scheme can be used to build curved hatch tops. The saw kerfs allow the hatch to bend in an arc. For hatch slides, dado pieces of dimensional teak and attach a Taco sliding extrusion for a smooth slider.

For hatches on the foredeck and cabintop, use two sets of hatch hinges, placed forward and aft, so that the hatch can be raised in either direction, allowing for the best ventilation by acting as a wind scoop.

To reinforce the hatch opening, I use a two-part carlin system. Before the decks are laminated into place, beams are installed to define the perimeter of the opening. The deck is then glued and fas-

tened over the framing. After the decks have been sheathed, the hatch opening is cut out, a task easily accomplished if you first drill small pilot holes from below, up through the deck at each of the four corners. Frame the opening with hatch carlins fastened directly into the framework. The hatch cover overlaps the carlins, and with a bit of foam-tape weather stripping on its bottom edges, it works very well. For offshore sailing, you might fit another wooden framework around the outside of the hatch; generously scuppered, this functions as a wave break and protects the hatch.

DOORS

For stowage areas too large or too visible for pigeon hole access, you may have to build cabinet doors. Most of the cabinets in our stitch-and-glue boats are built from sheets of plywood that run into corner blocks at their edges. This way, the plywood removed from the cutout in the cabinet front can be returned to its place of origin as a cabinet door. If you keep track of the cutouts, your doors will even match the grain of the surrounding bulkheads. Flat hinges seem to

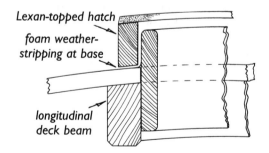

Figure 23-11. Hatch carlin system for a Lexan hatch.

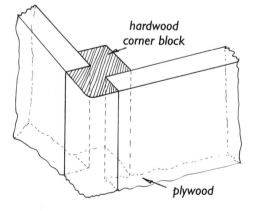

Figure 23-12. Corner blocking for a cabinet.

work best if they are screwed or bolted through the door casing.

For companionway doors, I stick to three choices: drop slides for sailboats, sliding doors for pilothouse boats, and hinged doors for boats without room for a sliding door. Each has advantages and disadvantages. Drop slides for a sailboat companionway are probably the easiest, strongest, and safest alternative. Cut the door shape out of the bulkhead. Frame the opening with hardwood slides, tapering the sides of the opening slightly (about ½ inch narrower at the bottom than at the top). Be sure to taper the interior edge of the hardwood strips to allow the plywood cutouts to slide easily; if you don't, the drop slides jam and stick.

Cut the drop boards into easily handled sizes, with a 45-degree bevel in the joints between boards to keep rainwater out of the boat. Be sure to scupper the bottom gutter so the slides don't sit in a pool of water.

On pilothouse boats I make sliding doors whenever possible. They work well if the sliding apparatus is at the top of the door. When a door slides on a bottom track, it always seems to stick and jam. With the sliding mechanism on top, the bottom track simply keeps the bottom of the door from swinging out. Usually there's not enough beam in the boat to remove the door by sliding it out at one end, so make the door track removable by removing the screws in the

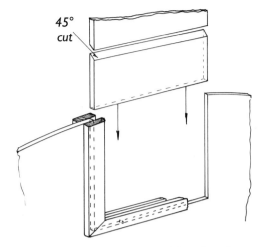

Figure 23-13. Drop slides and drop boards.

upper sliding track. Taco Metals #A52-0037 aluminum extrusion is available in 12-foot lengths and can be cut and shipped by UPS in shorter lengths. I use #40-601 WN nylon slides in the track. Use the bulkhead cutout for the door blank, and frame the door with 1½-inch-square stock dadoed out for the bulkhead thickness.

I use a similar concept for hinged doors by building a hardwood jamb around the bulkhead door cutout. You want to be sure the finished door is larger than the cutout, so use a mitered trim around the perimeter of the cutout just as you might have for the interior cabinet doors. Hang the door with removable hinges to allow unshipping in nice weather.

24

PAINTING

My preference for finishing surfaces is to paint all the exterior, except such trim as rubrails and toerails, and varnish all the interior, except for the overheads.

CHOICES OF PAINT SYSTEMS

For a stitch-and-glue boat, you have four basic classes of paints to choose from:

Alkyd enamel paints are all single-component, oil-based paint systems. You may be familiar with them already, because they're the enamel paints used in houses for porches and decks.

Epoxy paints are the distant cousins of the epoxy system with which you assembled your stitch-and-glue boat.

Acrylic urethane paints are two-part systems. They're very close relatives of the paint on your new car.

Linear polyurethane (LPU) paints are also two-part systems, but they're harder and more durable than the acrylic urethanes.

For your purposes, I would avoid the alkyd enamels, as their compatibility with epoxies is questionable. I do believe you could choose a paint from this family and use it successfully, but you'd be lucky to strike it right first time. It often appears that there are chemicals in alkyd enamels that react badly with the epoxy systems used for the boat's structure. The most common complaint is that alkyd enamels applied over epoxy take longer than normal to cure—or will not harden at all.

The best chance of success comes when you coat the boat with a conversion primer coat before painting with alkyd enamel. I would use several rolled-on or sprayed coats of epoxy DP primer for this conversion coating. More about this primer follows later in this chapter.

While the alkyd enamels don't always like the boatbuilding epoxy resin system, the epoxy DP primer seems quite compatible. Still, all in all I would avoid the alkyds as they are not a certain path to success.

An additional word of warning here. There is another class of paints called single-pack polyurethane coatings, or oil-modified polyurethane. While the paint manufacturers may refer to them as polyurethanes, you should be well aware that they are not the same thing as linear polyurethanes, which cure by the interlinking of molecules in a chemical reaction. In short, for topside paints I'd advise you to avoid any paint or clear covering that doesn't require the mixing of two parts.

Epoxy paints work very well as primers and conversion coats, but they're not the best for final coatings. Their biggest problem is that they chalk quite noticeably outdoors. The surface oxidizes somewhat and if you rub the weathered paint surface your finger will come away with a powdery coating of pigment.

For this reason, I don't recommend your using an epoxy-based paint system for your final surface coating—unless you approach the whole concept with your eyes wide open. I add this because, depending on your personal requirements, there is a case to be made for paints that chalk. It's practical, even if it isn't very "yachty." Commercial fishermen do it, and you can bet your life they don't spend any more time or money on upkeep than they have to—yet they want to protect their boats as well as they can. I'll have more to say about this in a bit.

The acrylic urethanes are hard and durable, and quite easy to touch up when damaged. I use a lot of them in my shop, the two most common being PPG's Deltron and Concept. Both are as easy to spray as any you'll find, and both give consistently good results.

The downside to Deltron and Concept is that they have to be sprayed. And spraying a finish is, in its own way, just as complicated as building boats. And bear in mind that these acrylic urethanes contain isocyanates. That means they're quite dangerous to your health if you breathe the fumes. When you're spraying these paints, organic vapor respirators offer only minimal protection. It's better to have a piped supply of pressurized fresh air for your face mask.

Linear polyurethanes, or LPUs, are the highest order of evolution of paint finishes. They can be quite finicky to apply, and they perform best when sprayed, although the best manufacturers offer special formulations for rolling or brushing as well. LPUs work very nicely over epoxy resins, with or without a conversion coating of epoxy primer. You should get very good results if you follow closely the manufacturer's recommendations and do all the groundwork necessary.

But they're thin, hard coatings, and they're so glossy that they'll show every little imperfection in the surface they're covering. However, that glossiness translates into long-term durability, so if you can manage to apply a coating of LPU satisfactorily, you'll have a paint system that will last as long as any possibly can in a marine environment.

Incidentally, LPUs also contain isocyanate, and must be handled with great care. In my shop, we pipe in fresh air from outside. The system comprises an oil-less compressor and hoses from there into the paint sprayer's face mask. It's very important to avoid any contact with the vapors or the paint itself. We use disposable Tyvek suits, disposable gloves, and a full-face mask air system.

In my shop, we do more spraying than hand-painting because it's faster if you know what you're doing. In the case of a non-professional, though, I don't believe it's worthwhile accumulating the experience you need to spray paint. So your best option is to use a paint system that allows for application by hand.

The best way to do this is to roll and brush. Properly done, this takes two people working side by side, both well protected with respirators. One rolls on the paint in sections of roughly 24 inches to 30 inches square. The other uses a foam, throwaway brush to tip off the freshly rolled paint with long even strokes. The idea is that the roller evenly applies paint without runs, and the brush smoothes out the roller stipple pattern.

Apply a thin coat of paint and plan on two coats. The final result can be very near professional spray quality. You'll have to work fast and be organized, but painting this way can be done by persons with very little experience.

One other possibility when it comes to painting with LPUs is to prepare the boat as completely as possible and then hire a professional painter to finish the job. There are quite a few people out there with experience of painting cars and trucks who have the equipment to do a good job for you. In the long run, it will be money well spent.

EXTERIOR SURFACES

The exterior of the boat is the main surface that is going to take the brunt of the abuse from weather and docking. What we need here is an easy-to-manage surface that will be hard and durable enough to absorb the knocks of daily use and still look good.

Painting is, of course, one of the last stages of building a boat and I find myself developing a love-hate relationship with the boat. I'm always happy to be done with the construction work, but I know from

experience that there's a long road still ahead.

On a 22-foot boat such as our Surf Scoter, we're talking about eight days of work, including primer coats—and that's when I spray rather than using a roller and brush. And during that session I will almost always run into trouble that calls for a re-spray.

What I need is a paint system with reliable, predictable characteristics, so I can use it whether it's 32° or 90°F outside. It should set up or cure quickly, to avoid having the shop shut down any longer than necessary. It should be good and durable, and it should look like a million dollars.

But what I need isn't always what I get. It's not easy to combine all these fine qualities in one paint system. What it boils down to in the end is either acrylic urethanes or linear polyurethanes (LPUs). For roller-and-brush application, as stated above, choose LPUs. You may be acquainted with the names of a couple of LPUs. Awlgrip and Sterling are two of the best-known. Both of them have formulations for application by hand as well as by spray gun.

If you're feeling adventurous, you can always experiment. I finished one of my beach cruisers with an epoxy primer that normally acts as an undercoat for other paint systems. It's made by the Ditzler Paint Company, a division of PPG Paint. Called DP Primer, it comes in black, white, gray, green-gray, and red oxide. It's a two-part system and cures in any weather. You can spray it, brush it, or roll it on.

These DP Primer paints are classed as "non-topcoat type," because they don't necessarily have to be covered with a top-coat for a durable finish. Their own finish is hard and durable, and can easily be

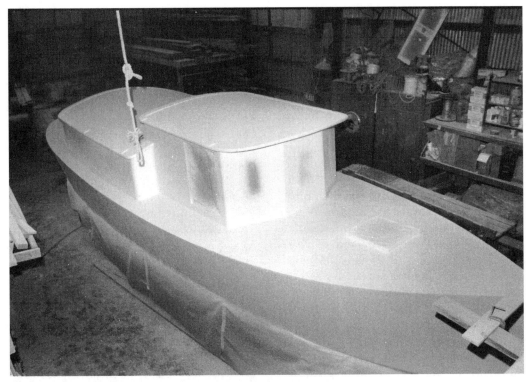

Figure 24-1. Paint work underway on Czarinna, a 35-foot, twin-screw powerboat. Most of the woodwork has been finished, and all the freshly painted areas have been masked off. Pilothouse windows will be cut out once painting is completed.

painted over later on if necessary. DP Primers give a smart satin surface that doesn't emphasize minor imperfections as a glossy finish does.

The beach cruiser was 28 feet long and 6 feet wide, powered by a 10-horse inboard diesel. I painted the hull DP white. The decks and cockpit were DP gray. If you're prepared to forgo the traditional glossy yacht finish, you could use a DP system like the beach cruiser's and save yourself a lot of preparation and finishing time.

My confidence in the DP Primer system has increased over the years. It's the base paint that has gone on my duckboats for more than 10 years. DP Primer will chalk a bit as it ages—a tendency of all epoxy-based paints—but it doesn't seem to compromise their durability.

However, having said that, I realize that the urge to put a perfectly smooth, glossy surface on your boat can be quite overwhelming. So I guess we'd better discuss how to accomplish that goal.

Protecting your Epoxy

One of the best reasons to paint as much of the exterior of your boat as possible is to protect the epoxy sealing and sheathing of the wood from degradation by ultraviolet rays from the sun. The epoxy with which your boat is built, and which it relies upon for its strength, does not have any natural protection from the sun's rays.

For that matter, if we continue to deplete the ozone layer, human beings won't have any protection from ultraviolet rays either. Just as we must protect ourselves with sunscreens, so we must protect the epoxy. The best way to do this is to cover it with paint, which is opaque. But if you want a clear, varnish-like finish, you must cover the epoxy-sealed wood with a varnish or other clear coating that contains ultraviolet filters. And, because no clear finish can block ultraviolet rays as efficiently as paint, all clear coatings must be renewed annually to provide adequate protection for the epoxy.

If this sounds like a lot of work, it is. So be very careful when you consider finishing a part of your boat as brightwork. You can spend an awful lot of time keeping that finish up.

Epoxy is such a magic material that people sometimes find it difficult to believe how susceptible it is to sunlight. But degradation is fast and deadly. You can see this for yourself in a simple experiment.

Coat a piece of plywood with epoxy resin and allow it to cure. Place it outside where sunlight can reach it. Place another piece of plywood over at least a half of the coated piece. After just a couple of days, have a look at your sample. The part that was covered will be quite a different color from the part that was exposed to the sun.

The Effect of Paint Color

Another good reason why you put finish coatings on your boat is to protect the epoxy from heat damage. If you paint your boat a dark color, such as blue, green, or black, you can actually shorten its life. Epoxy resins can be quite heat-sensitive and it's best to keep them as cool as possible.

I don't come across this problem much here in the Pacific Northwest, but I still find that a dark-painted boat requires at least twice as much attention to stay looking good as its lighter-colored sistership.

The color of the paint makes a difference in surface temperature of as much as 40°F on a sunny day. My own boat, an Arctic Tern, 22-foot 8-inch sailboat, was originally a light gray. After four years, the original paint was in good condition, but my curiosity got the better of me and I painted her a dark blue. Very smart, but . . . .

A year later, during her annual haulout, I looked closely at the hull surface. When she was gray, the hull was fair and smooth. Now I could see the pattern of the fiberglass sheathing showing through, or telegraphing, in the topsides. The only difference was the color, and one year of being heated by the sun.

So I conducted an experiment on a 92°F day. I placed a thermometer on the dark-blue topsides and got a recording of 142°. I then placed the thermometer on a nearby surface painted off-white. It registered 113 degrees. Quite a difference.

Now epoxy resin can have a heat deflection temperature of about 125°F. That's the temperature at which cured epoxy begins to deflect, or move, under stress. It can also have a glass transition temperature—the temperature at which cured epoxy begins to behave more like a rubber compound than like hard epoxy—of about 150°F. So an epoxy-built boat painted in dark colors is very much operating in a range of temperatures that could have rather frightening consequences.

My experience with boats with dark exteriors is that they exhibit, to various degrees, the following traits:

First, they have a noticeable tendency to show print-through—the pattern of the fiberglass cloth underneath. They will also show raised grain in the hull surface.

Second, they will show quite clearly any scarf joint in the plywood, and any interruption in the wood grain or pattern of the various components of the hull. They will emphasize filled fastening holes, corner blocks, and any joint in the structure.

Let me make it clear that what we're talking about here is looks, not structural integrity. I have never seen a total structural failure of a stitch-and-glue epoxy composite boat caused by the color of the paint. It's just that if your paint job is dark, it will look in need of attention at least twice as quickly as a lighter boat will. As a matter of fact, even light surfaces will show some of the symptoms mentioned above, but to a far less noticeable degree.

The moral is that you could be wasting your time spending countless hours sanding and smoothing if you're going to paint your boat a dark color. You have to decide for yourself.

Of course, there are other causes, besides dark paint, of print-through or telegraphing in the hull surface. My own experience has uncovered the following fairly consistent causes of exaggerated telegraphing:

Painting a boat too soon after applying epoxy and glass. The epoxy should cure for at least a month, preferably two months.

Moving the freshly painted boat out into the hot sun too soon. Wait at least a month. The longer the paint cures, and the shorter the initial periods of exposure to sun, the better.

Building and painting in an unheated shop in winter. The cooler and more humid the weather, the more likely it is that the hull will show telegraphing.

Very thin coatings of primer and finish coat. Fatter coatings hide joints and patterns better.

Overcoating too soon. Allow a generous cure time between coats.

Using a soft, more flexible epoxy for the exterior sheathing. As a general rule, comparing a couple of well-known epoxy systems, the more hardener in the mix, the more flexible the system. It sounds paradoxical, but an epoxy with two parts of resin to one part of hardener would often be more flexible than another with five parts of resin to one part of hardener. The latter, less flexible epoxy system, will hide print-through better.

Another way to help reduce telegraphing is to post-cure the epoxy. This is an attempt to simulate the natural processes your boat will be subjected to in use, the heating and cooling cycles that help settle the epoxy into its final form.

Think of the environment your boat will be subjected to. That might mean freezing cold weather in winter and hot, humid weather in summer. It might also mean sudden changes, which can inflict more strain than longer, more gradual changes of temperature.

Your epoxy has to shrink and stretch to accommodate these extremes, and if you can mature it by putting it through its paces before you apply the final coats of paint, your chances of achieving perfection are much better.

One way to do this is to use infrared heaters during construction. I use a quartz infrared heater that I bought from the Grainger Co., and move it around the boat in 30-minute or longer sessions. Another method that I've been exploring is to use a black epoxy primer on boats small enough to move outside on a moderately sunny day, letting the sun do our heating work for us.

You can buy from your epoxy supplier some small strip thermometers to tape on to the surface of the hull. Be careful not to let the temperature exceed 140°F; but anything below that will be helpful in post-curing the epoxy.

Some epoxy manufacturers make special epoxy coatings that need to be post-cured in ovens, or perhaps with our black primer in sunshine, up to and in excess of 140°F. They can be very tough and strong, but my feeling is that amateurs had best leave them alone.

Secrets of a Perfect Paint Finish

Here are the steps you'll need to take to ensure perfection—or at least a smooth and fair finish:

Do the best and smoothest job you possibly can of glassing the hull.

Sand lightly, and after applying a layer of epoxy mixed with microballoons on the unfair glass overlaps, sand again.

Now reseal the entire structure with Cabosil-thickened epoxy resin. This layer will serve both to seal and to prime.

Lightly sand the hull with 80-grit sandpaper on a random orbit sander—no more grinding from here on in. Take care not to sand into the fiberglass cloth. If you do, reseal the area with another rolled-on coat of epoxy.

Now is the time to post-cure the surface with infrared heaters or sunshine. If you choose not to post-cure, move right along.

Roll on the first conversion coat of DP 40 epoxy primer and allow it to cure.

Now go around the hull looking for defects in the finish. Fill them with a mixture of epoxy resin and microballoons or Microlight fillers if they are deep, or with a lacquer glazing putty if they are shallow. This putty is available at an automotive paint store.

Sand the filled spots smooth with 150-grit sandpaper. If you used Microlight filler, you now need to reseal the surface with unthickened epoxy resin to ensure a uniformly smooth surface.

Sand the whole hull again to a matte surface with 150-grit paper.

If you're now happy with surface, and you have managed to maintain the epoxy primer on most of the surface, you can sand the entire boat with 220-grit paper and prepare for the final paint coats.

But if you find the surface still needs some work, you'll have to re-prime. We use an easily sanded primer called K36 Prima, made by PPG. Prima likes to be sprayed, but you can use the roll-and-brush technique mentioned earlier.

Sand the surface with 220-grit paper and you should be very close to perfection. Any remaining flaws should require only minor filling with glazing putty. Sand the putty smooth with 220-grit paper also.

Now apply a final coat of DP 40 primer

as a sealer and primer for the final coats. The need here is for a smooth surface devoid of any areas of porosity. If you roll-and-brush this last layer of primer, you will want to allow it to cure at least overnight.

Then sand it very lightly with 220- or 320-grit paper, depending on how fine a finish you want, and you're ready to apply the final paint coats.

If you sprayed the DP 40, allow it to cure for at least three hours. Then, without sanding, go into your final sprayed-finish enamels.

If you're spraying on the final coats, you'll need at least three medium-coverage coats with at least one hour between each coat. That's time enough for the underlying layers to cure without causing a problem with solvent entrapment.

If you're rolling and brushing your final coats, you'll need to apply a coat of normal thickness and let it cure—at least overnight. Then scuff it lightly with a 3M Scotchbrite pad, and apply another coat the next day.

Some Useful Rules

In my shop I have set some rules for the application of all two-component epoxy, acrylic, or polyurethane paints. The first is to use *exactly* the proper ratio of paint to catalyst. Always follow the paint manufacturer's recommendations in every respect.

The second rule is that you cannot overstir the paint-and-catalyst mixture. After stirring adequately, as instructed by the manufacturer, let the mixture sit, or induct, and then stir it again after several minutes. Don't let the instructions on the

can mislead you into thinking that no induction time is needed. It is.

The third rule is always to strain the mixed and inducted paint before using it. You'd be surprised what will show up in the strainer sometimes. Fourth, always "push," or accelerate, the paint to the limit suggested by the manufacturer. The faster it sets up, the better for the project and the less chance for contamination.

The fifth rule is to avoid any contact with LPU. Don't breathe it, don't touch it. I've mentioned it before, and I mean it. I use solvent-proof gloves, Tyvek spray suits, barrier cream on my face and particularly around my eyes, a spray sock over my head, and a separate fresh-air system blowing in filtered air from outside the shop. Goggles are important, or some kind of safety glasses, to prevent sprayback getting into your eyes. A full-face mask unit for a fresh air system is a good idea, too. LPUs and acrylics contain isocyanates. That's part of what makes them beautiful and durable. That's also what makes them killers.

The sixth rule is not to use sandpaper that's too smooth. Most two-component paints need a little "tooth" to hang on to. I have found it best to stop at 320-grit sandpaper for most paint systems, and in a lot of cases 220-grit will suffice.

Rule seven is to use tack cloths before painting to remove every last trace of dust from the sanded surface.

Finally, some food for thought. The adhesion of the coat of paint you're applying is only as good as the adhesion of the undercoats. It may seem redundant even to mention this, but I've seen painters who believed that two-component paints were some magic form of glue that would help flaking undercoats stick themselves to the boat. Forget it. All you'll have is a coat of paint over loose layers of marginal undercoats, ready to peel off at the first decent bump.

APPLYING NON-SKID SURFACES

You can apply non-skid finishes by hand or by spray gun. Let's first look at how to do it by hand.

You apply non-skid after you've done the smooth painting on the deck and cockpit surfaces. Let the paint cure for at least two days. Then define the perimeters of your non-skid areas with masking tape.

Lightly sand the non-skid areas with 220-grit sandpaper until you have a uniformly matte surface with no glossy spots showing. For best paint adhesion you should always sand between layers, and for the final finish coat you can Scotchbrite between layers.

Now mix up the non-skid paint of your choice. Make quite sure you've mixed both components thoroughly before you add the recommended percentage of non-skid compound. If you're like me, you'll stir in an extra 25 percent of non-skid. That gives you a slightly higher profile non-skid.

You can roll this paint mixture on, but keep reminding yourself to stir it very frequently to ensure even coverage. Apply at least two coats to get the right texture, and don't bother to brush out the stipple in this case. Wait for about two hours between coats. Remove your masking tape as soon as you can do so *and* leave a neat edge. If you forget, and leave it to bake on overnight, you'll be very, very sorry, as the paint will creep under the masking tape and leave a rough edge.

You can also sprinkle non-skid additive over a freshly rolled-on coat of paint to create non-skid. Be sure to vacuum off the excess non-skid material before rolling on additional coats of paint to seal the non-skid compound.

Or you can mix up a paint and non-skid additive mixture and spray it on your surfaces. Several light coats done in multiple passes can yield the best results of all the non-skid application techniques.

INTERIOR FINISHES

My preference for interiors is an all-bright finish (that is, an all-clear finish) with a painted overhead. Painting the overhead a light color goes a long way toward reflecting light back into the interior. It keeps things feeling bright and airy. If you don't paint the overhead, the boat's interior can sometimes look pretty dark and oppressive.

I paint in advance the undersides of the cabin top and decks with the same type of system I'll be using on the rest of the interior before fastening them to the deck framing structure.

When painting in advance, I first seal the panels of plywood with epoxy resin. When that has set up, I sand with 220-grit paper and apply the coats of paint. The roll-and-brush method works well here, but it always takes two coats to give me the coverage I want.

After the paint has cured, I sand it lightly with 320-grit paper. The pre-painted panels are then cut to shape, and ready to apply. Incidentally, don't neglect to think the process through thoroughly—you need to have all plywood joints and seams in the finished overhead landing on structural framing.

For gluing on these pre-painted panels I use a white polyurethane bedding compound such as Sikaflex or 3M's 5200 compound. I fasten the overheads with screws into the deck framing and quickly clean off the squeezed-out bedding compound with clean rags and mineral spirits, and then continue with the balance of the deck and overhead layers, laminating with epoxy and screw-fastening into the framing.

Finally, I have surfaces that are painted, sanded, and at the same stage of finish as the rest of the interior. For the final finish I now spray several coats of clear acrylic urethane over the entire interior, both the epoxy-sealed brightwork and the painted overheads.

In one good day of spraying I can apply four to six coats of clear finish. I prefer to use a flatting agent mixed into a clear finish to create a satin appearance. I think a smooth glossy finish looks quite garish down below. It certainly doesn't suit my tastes.

I apply the flatted clear finish on every surface, including the pre-painted overheads. The result is a uniform, satin finish.

If you're applying your finishes by hand, you'll find you can achieve similar results with the roll-and-brush method, although it will take you much longer.

As with so many aspects of boatbuilding, preparation is everything to the final result. Make sure your surfaces are clean and dust-free. Lightly wet down the shop floor to help pull excess floating dust from the air. Use a tack rag just before painting or varnishing, and use clean, fresh rollers, brushes, paint-mixing tubs, and tools. The only other things you need are a lot of patience, and a similar amount of luck.

25

EXTERIOR TRIM AND HARDWARE

EXTERIOR TRIM

Toerails, rubrails, caprails, and other trim can make or break the appearance and finish of a boat. If the trim is out of scale, the boat will appear out of proportion. If the trim work is sloppy, the cosmetic effect will cheapen the overall quality of the boat.

All the trim on my boats shares one thing: It is all added after the basic boat is completed and painted. There are two reasons for delaying the trim until after the final painting. One is to achieve a uniform and fully protective paint job; the second is to minimize the tedious job of masking required before painting.

Each design has its own trim details and scantlings, but the basic procedure is the same: premachine the parts, dry fit them for accuracy, and finish the final sanding and prefinish (coatings) before installing them. My goal is to only minimally touch the trim after I've installed the pieces with screws or bolts, bunged the fastener holes, and chiseled the bungs off flush with the surface. Most of that fin-ish work is to simply apply another couple of coats of oil, Cetol, or varnish to seal the bungs.

It is becoming increasingly difficult to buy long lengths of mahogany and teak to use for exterior trim, so the alternative is to scarf the stock to appropriate lengths. When scarfing, always consider the run of the grain in the piece of trim, and align the scarfs so they shingle past obstructions instead of catching them (see Figure 25-1).

Rainwater and splash will run across decks, course over the top edge of a rubrail, and sheet down the topsides, discoloring the topsides paint. To prevent this, cut a drip groove about ⅛ inch wide and ¼ inch deep in the lower edge of a rubrail.

Place fasteners at least every 6 inches along the length of the trim, and always bed the trim in a polyurethane caulking compound. The woods of choice are teak for varnished, Cetoled, or oiled trim, and mahogany for trim that is more cosmetic and either varnished or epoxied and var-nished. Oak and locust are excellent choices, too, if you can find them. Whatever wood you choose, bear in mind that the first purpose of trim is to bear

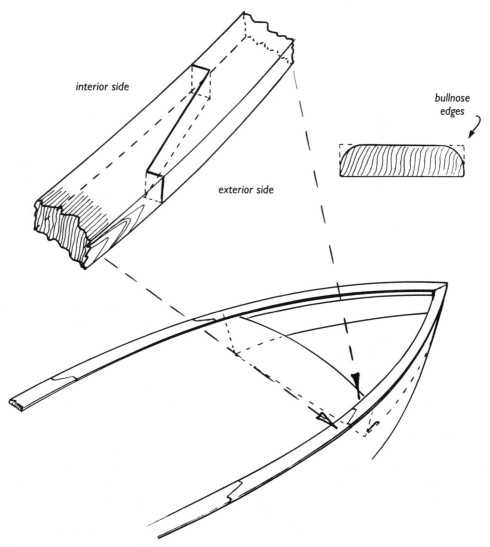

Figure 25-1. Align scarfs so they shingle past obstructions instead of catching them.

chafe, so consider how the wood will stand up over the long run: Will it stain dark when damaged or scuffed? Will those blemishes affect the overall appearance of the boat? I generally shy away from the light blond oak or locust woods for that reason, opting for the darker mahogany or teak.

Exterior trim, such as handrails and steps, should always be made of tough hardwood. Teak is ideal because it withstands neglect better than most other woods, and when oiled always looks good. Safety aids such as handrails should be through-bolted whenever possible.

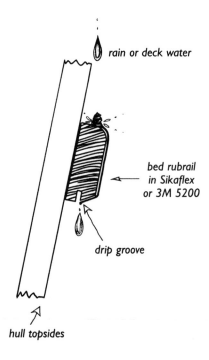

rain or deck water

bed rubrail
in Sikaflex
or 3M 5200

drip groove

hull topsides

Figure 25-2. A saw-cut drip groove in the rubrail will prevent topsides discoloration.

HARDWARE

The hardware you install on your boat will have to appeal to your own sense of aesthetics above all else. Beyond that, it should be practical and affordable. I prefer to use plain bronze whenever possible, and I don't polish it because I prefer the light-green patina of oxidized bronze. However, there are some things that just are not available in bronze, and in such cases I use stainless steel.

When you use stainless steel, use the hi_hest grade available. Type 304 (sometimes referred to as 18-8) is good, but type 316 is much more resistant to crevice corrosion. Type 304 will appear to rust and

look less than shipshape after a while. If you buy stainless steel hardware, look for smooth and polished surfaces to reduce the problems of crevice corrosion. When used underwater, stainless steel is particularly vulnerable to crevice corrosion; better to confine its use above the waterline or inside the boat.

All marine hardware is frighteningly expensive, but there is no substitution. Nonmarine hardware just doesn't hold up as well. You've come this far in the building project, and you owe it to yourself to finish your boat off with the best hardware available.

Coat and seal the edges of all hardware-fastening holes with epoxy. I keep a supply of pipe cleaners to coat the interiors of the smaller holes. Any breach in the epoxy sealing will later come back to haunt you, so be thorough.

Use through-bolts to mount hardware whenever possible, and make sure high-load items such as cleats and mooring bitts have bronze or stainless steel backing plates. One-eighth-inch silicon bronze plate stock works well for customized backing plates. It drills much easier than stainless steel and can be cut with a jigsaw or bandsaw with a dull wood-cutting blade. Bed the hardware with polyurethane bedding compound, and wipe off the excess caulk with a clean rag and mineral spirits.

I use stainless steel bolts with nylon-insert, aircraft-type nuts for attaching most hardware. These nuts don't need lock washers and won't back off the threads as the boat ages. Use large flat washers or backing plates to help spread the load over as large a surface as possible, and bed the hardware meticulously. If you've got room, use the larger-diameter fender washers to help through-bolt backup loads.

26

PROPULSION

How you power a boat has everything to do with the ultimate enjoyment of the craft. Gone are the days when boats were either human-powered or sail-powered. Today, even if you are building a sailboat you cannot ignore the need for mechanical propulsion as a backup system.

Do you need redundant or spare power for your boat? I think the answer will have to be addressed by each individual. In my own sailboat, a 23-foot Arctic Tern, I have a 10-hp diesel inboard auxiliary. With the sails, the diesel, and a good anchor, I can probably deal with most problems that might come up. Insist on a good, reliable power plant, adequate ground tackle, and a VHF radio to help you if the worst comes to pass. And maintain the engine religiously. If you neglect engine maintenance, expect bad karma; she will indeed let you down when you might need her most.

Although stitch-and-glue designs have no special inboard or outboard power requirements, I have developed some methods that make inboard engine installation a little easier. Engine beds are the first issue. You will need to do a bit of lay-out work to accommodate the shaft and engine bed angles. Generally, modern marine engines require the motor mounts to be in line (parallel) with the propeller shaft angle. Cut an oblong hole in the keel of the boat at the expected position of the packing box; the hole will help locate the shaft line. Stretch a string from the position of the aftmost strut or shaft bearing to help measure the shaft angle. The engine manufacturer will indicate the maximum allowable shaft angle, usually not more than 15 degrees from the level waterline. Inside the engine room, attach the string along the centerline of the shaft to the front of the engine room. If your string cannot stretch straight, you'll need to redrill the hole cut in the bilge. Be careful not to overbore this hole.

Make a cross-frame jig and attach it to the forward engine box wall or a bulkhead forward of where the engine is going to be mounted. Adjust the jigs and the string until the shaft angle is correct and the stern bearing is in proper relationship to the hull. (A Smartlevel is a real time-saver, electronically showing angles as held up to the string.)

Vernay Products Inc. of Thomasville,

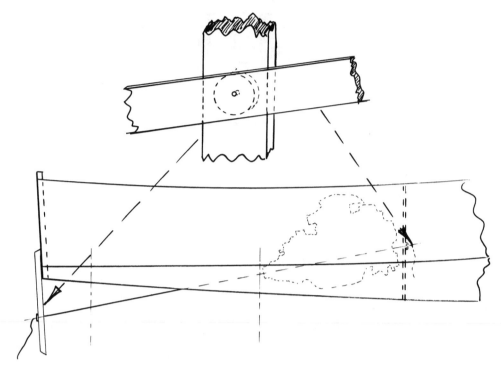

Figure 26-1. A string stretched at the proper angles will help line up the shaft log.

Georgia, manufactures an excellent premade fiberglass shaft tube. Made by a filament winding process, these strong fiberglass tubes can be easily bonded into a stitch-and-glue boat. After determining the appropriate tube size for your engine installation, enlarge the hole in the bilge so you can slip the tube through the bottom of the boat at the proper shaft angle. Bond the tube in place with high-density epoxy fillets, making sure the shaft is centered at each end and aligned with the string. On a fin-keeled sailboat, you'll want the tube to extend slightly past the bottom of the boat. Glass the interior and exterior with epoxy and several layers of biaxial tape. If your boat has a wooden full keel, like the Surf Scoter, install the shaft tube by glassing where it exits into the inside of the boat

only. The outside of the tube will extend through the keel in a notch cutout. The Surf Scoter calls for a tube of 2-inch outside diameter and 1½-inch inside diameter.

Once the shaft tube has been glassed in place, the engine beds can be installed. For small diesel engines, the engine mounts are usually parallel to the shaft, although on certain models they may be as much as 1 inch above or below the shaft line. With ¼-inch plywood template stock, make a pattern for the engine mounts. Then, taking careful measurements of the angle from the boat's bottom, laminate the engine beds from four layers of high-quality ½-inch marine plywood. Depending on the shape of the hull and configuration of the motor box, the bed may decrease in height until it runs out aft or, in some cases, run up to the cockpit longitudinals once clear of the engine. The Surf Scoter bed has a ¾-inch bridge at the top, extending over to the sides of the engine box and becoming part of the cockpit longitudinal supports. This design allows several parts to serve double-duty and creates an extremely strong engine bed grid.

Sometimes, to avoid setting the flexible engine mounts directly on the wooden beds, I fabricate two slightly larger beds of stainless steel angle iron with nuts welded on the bottom. The engine mount bolts will screw down into these nuts, thus holding the engine securely onto the bed. The stainless steel beds fasten down over the inside edge of the wooden engine beds,

and they allow you one more opportunity for adjustment to proper alignment between the engine bed and shaft. If necessary, the stainless steel beds can be shimmed before being bolted solidly to the wooden engine beds.

Another helpful item toward a proper inboard installation is a flexible shaft log such as the type made by the Buck-Algonquin Company. The Surf Scoter uses an SL-125 FG for a 1¼-inch shaft. It looks like a bronze packing box connected to a heavy, thick piece of radiator hose. These packing boxes can be fastened to the end of the fiberglass stern tube with hose clamps, and are somewhat self-aligning because of the flexible nature of the radiator hose.

Figure 26-2. A proper set of engine beds in the 29-foot Means of Grace design. A horizontal flat will be bonded onto this bed port and starboard to complete the engine package. The whole area has received several coats of epoxy to seal it. Note the large round holes to access through-bolts on the engine mounts and to eliminate dead-air spaces.

27

LAUNCHING

Much like childbirth, launch day mixes pain with joy. It might seem that this boat you've invested so much time and money on is unwilling to start its life off the cradle. My most vivid mental image of a launch includes the builder chasing the boat down the ways with a paint brush to get that last coat of paint on the hull before it hits the water. No matter how hard I try to get all the prelaunch jobs done, a few always seem to slip through the cracks and pop up on launch day. At some point, the builder must say: "No more paint! No more varnish! No more woodwork!" Otherwise, even the smallest and simplest boat could be worked on forever. Launch day usually occurs just after my mood has bottomed out and is on its way up again. The corner is turned when I finally resolve not to do that extra work, but to shove the boat through the shop door. We've got a saying that goes, "You've got to hate 'em to finish 'em." That is, you need some sort of motivation to finish the boat, and that motivation may be a momentary type of loathing.

Launch celebrations run the gamut from large parties with hired bands to low-key splashes with barely a few words of ded-

ication. I like the story about how some African boatbuilders used to launch their dugout canoes. The boatbuilder would not actually attend the launch, but instead would conceal himself nearby, within earshot. There he would wait for the crowd's response to the launch. If he heard cries of joy he would go and join the party, but if he heard groans and curses of sorrow and derision he would bolt to a good head start on his angry pursuers, knowing that after a few weeks he could return to less impassioned feelings, and start the next boat.

If you are going to have a formal party, launch the boat twice, the first time as a dress rehearsal (a builder's launch) without spectators. Crank the engines, rig the sails, and work through the boat's systems. Satisfy yourself that everything's in working order. There's plenty of stress at a launch party; you don't need to add to it by having to troubleshoot the boat at the last minute. Then when you're satisfied she is not going to embarrass you, go through the formal launch—this one's for the owner now and you can give it the full attention it deserves.

Some people want long dedications,

others don't. My only consistent remark for every boat is, "Over the land and into the drink, please God, don't let it sink!" It might be that I'll say it out loud or I might mutter it under my breath. The point is, the work ends only when the launch is successfully over, the boat's tied up securely to a mooring or a dock, and I'm back home with my feet up hoisting a few to the memories of the others that preceded it.

28

REPAIRS

Stitch-and-glue boats are remarkably tough and resilient. I have seen only one boat come back for a major repair in all my years of boat construction. It was a 22-foot Surf Scoter powerboat, and I was aware of the problem even before the owner called me.

The winter of 1990–91 was unusually tough in the Pacific Northwest, marked by more rain than anyone could remember. In just two days, we received over 16 inches, accompanied by several huge wind storms. On one of those evenings after work, I was watching the news and saw a story about a marina that was being assaulted by a particularly fierce north wind. The wave action was so intense that the marina's breakwater was destroyed. Television cameras panned the watery chaos as boats were bounced about, some thrown onto the beach. People were trying to hold their boats away from the rocks with their hands and feet. In the midst of this I noticed a flash of green bouncing in and out of sight, and recognized it as one of my Surf Scoters.

The boatowner called a couple of days later to report the whole story. His boat had been tied to the main stem of the dock leading out from shore. Off the main dock were a number of smaller finger piers. When the breakwater started to fail, debris drifted down on the finger piers, which eventually broke away from the main trunk. All in all, approximately 30 boats were sunk, 30 were partially submerged, and another 40 were pushed up onto the beach where the surf took care of them.

Our poor Surf Scoter remained tied to the main dock along with eight other boats. Broken cement docks with jagged edges and steel rebar projecting at waterline level floated down onto the boats, chewing into the Surf Scoter's hull. A fishing boat had drifted into the Surf Scoter and ground away at the topsides. The resulting damage was a severely chafed and gouged stern, holes punched into the waterline on the port side (thankfully the holes that penetrated went into the ballast water tanks), and a large hole through the port topsides, just above the galley, that looked like a new porthole from the inside. The stem was badly damaged just above the waterline where the boat had surged against the cement dock, chafing through a $\frac{3}{16}$-inch-thick, $\frac{1}{2}$-inch-wide brass

Figure 28-1. The stem of a tortured Surf Scoter after a big Puget Sound storm in 1990. Many of this boat's neighbors were sunk during the same storm.

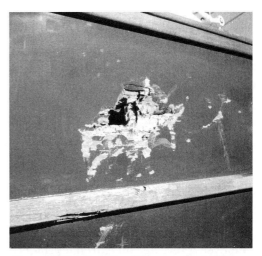

Figure 28-2. The side of the same boat. The gillnet fishing boat that did this damage ultimately sank in the storm.

half-oval on the stem and a 2-inch by 6-inch timber chafe strip on the dock.

The day after the storm, the owner's wife ran the boat 10 miles across a bay to the nearest haulout facility. A couple of weeks later I looked the boat over to make an estimate of the repair costs, and not long afterward towed the boat back to my shop for repairs.

It was a great opportunity to open up a boat to see how it was holding up. The Surf Scoter was about four years old at the time of repair, and I could find no evidence of discoloration in the wood to indicate moisture invasion; best of all, the epoxy sealing on both sides of the hull panels looked as good as new.

The stem was the easiest to repair. We cut away the damaged material down to good wood, and then shaped a wood dutchman to fill the cutout, gluing it in place with epoxy.

Turning to the new port-side "port-

hole," I cut out the damaged area with a router to enlarge the hole into sound, undamaged wood, then routed the perimeter about halfway through the ½-inch-thick hull side, creating a "stepped" opening. Two ¼-inch plywood patches were cut: one to fit into the hole, and a second, slightly larger one to fit into the routed shelf around the hole. I glued the largest in first, fastening through the narrow flange around the hole. After the glue dried, I glued and fastened the smaller patch into place, bringing the repair flush with the hull's interior and exterior surfaces. To hide the repair in the varnished interior surface, I cut a long butt-block panel to cover it. The galley countertop was reinstalled in its original position, and with the butt block in place, the patch looked like part of the original construction.

On the exterior, the repair and surrounding painted area of the hull were sanded until the glass cloth layers were visible. The patch was ground to $\frac{1}{16}$-inch below the surrounding surface level of the original hull. Two pieces of 6-ounce fiberglass cloth, one covering just the patch and the other cut larger to overlap the hull 6 inches on all sides of the patch, were laminated in place with epoxy and peel ply. A light sanding and a coat of microballoon/epoxy fairing compound leveled the repair surfaces. To save a little time and effort, I covered the fairing compound with 2-inch-wide clear cellophane packing tape, then smoothed the tape with a squeegee. When the tape was later removed it revealed an extremely smooth patch. (The tape also holds the filler material firmly in place on vertical surfaces, preventing sags.) All that remained was to prime and paint the repair. The Surf Scoter was repaired with about 90 hours of labor, most of which was taken up in the complete stem-to-stern exterior repainting of the boat. The patches were easy to do and involved no more skill than any other part of the stitch-and-glue construction process.

I am periodically asked about designing a boat for extended cruising in cold, hostile waters. This type of cruising intrigues me. I have always been drawn to remote and desolate places, and my efforts in designing include materials that will fare well in extreme conditions.

Steel is resilient, aluminum allows freedom from paint and concern for corrosion, and fiberglass is strong. But, welding patches of steel does not appeal to me, I detest the cold gray color of unpainted aluminum, and I can't see carrying a TIG welder with me to facilitate patches. A fiberglass boat would need to be epoxied if damaged, and its interior would need to be covered with wood or fabric ceiling to avoid condensation problems in a cold environment.

I believe the wooden stitch-and-glue boat is the best answer. A wood boat doesn't sweat, so you could have a hull in which all interior surfaces were visible and easily accessible. In the event of hull damage, precut plywood patches with waterproof polyurethane caulking at the edges and some bronze ring-shanked boat nails or screws are all you'd need to quickly fasten a temporary patch over most any hole. And with wood's relatively light-weight-to-high-strength ratio, a stitch-and-glue hull would rate better than most at being a good shipmate in extreme conditions.

APPENDIX A

DEVLIN'S DESIGNS

Here is a sampling of designs available from the Devlin shop. A 100-page catalog detailing 43 stitch-and-glue designs is available for $10 by writing or calling:

Devlin Designing Boat Builders
2424 Gravelly Beach Loop, N.W.
Olympia, WA 98520
(360) 866-0164, FAX (360) 866-4548

CACKLER

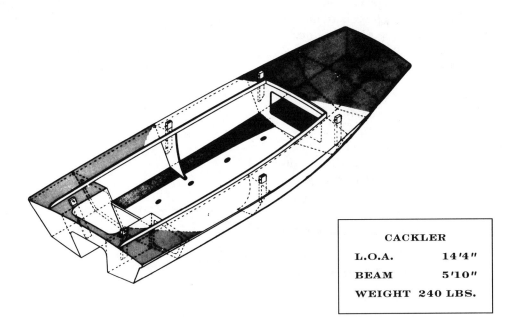

CACKLER	
L.O.A.	14'4"
BEAM	5'10"
WEIGHT	240 LBS.

POLLIWOG

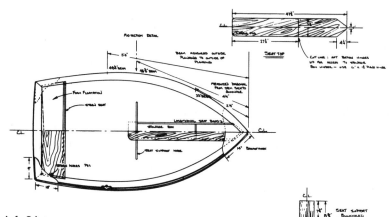

Pollywog Materials List

2 sheets	4 x 8-foot, ¼-inch plyood
12 feet	mahogany, 1 x 12 inches
1 gallon	epoxy resin
½ gallon	epoxy hardener
1 roll (50 yards)	4-inch x 8-ounce fiberglass cloth
7 yards	38-inch x 6-ounce fiberglass cloth
2 pounds	wood flour
2 quarts	primer
1 pint	varnish
1 quart	enamel
2	#4482 Wilcox Crittendon oarlock sockets

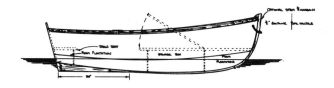

POLLIWOG	
L.O.A.	7'6"
BEAM	4'1"
WEIGHT	59 LBS.

PEEPER

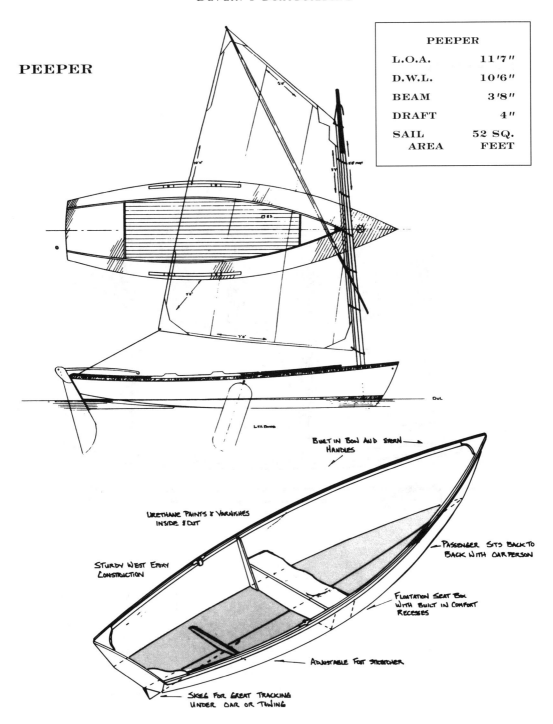

PEEPER	
L.O.A.	11'7"
D.W.L.	10'6"
BEAM	3'8"
DRAFT	4"
SAIL AREA	52 SQ. FEET

BUILT IN BOW AND STERN HANDLES

URETHANE PAINTS & VARNISHES INSIDE & OUT

STURDY WEST EPOXY CONSTRUCTION

PASSENGER SITS BACK TO BACK WITH OAR PERSON

FLOATATION SEAT BOX WITH BUILT IN COMFORT RECESSES

ADJUSTABLE FOOT STRETCHER

SKEG FOR GREAT TRACKING UNDER OAR OR TOWING

SEA SWIFT

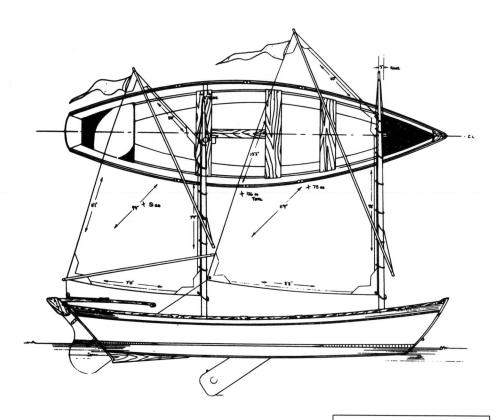

SEA SWIFT	
L.O.A.	19'3"
L.W.L.	15'9"
BEAM	5'5"
DRAFT	6"
3'6" WITH THE BOARD DOWN	
SAIL AREA	126 SQ. FEET

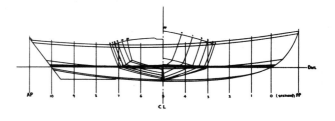

NANCY'S CHINA

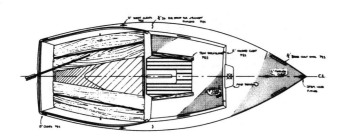

NANCY'S CHINA		
L.O.A.		**15'2"**
L.W.L.		**12'6"**
BEAM		**6'0"**
DRAFT (UP)		**0'10"**
(DOWN)		**2'9"**
SAIL		**112 SQ.**
AREA		**FEET**

NANCY'S CHINA DC

NANCY'S CHINA DC	
L.O.A.	15'2"
BEAM	6'2"
DRAFT (UP)	10"
(DOWN)	2'9"
SAIL AREA	124 SQ. FEET

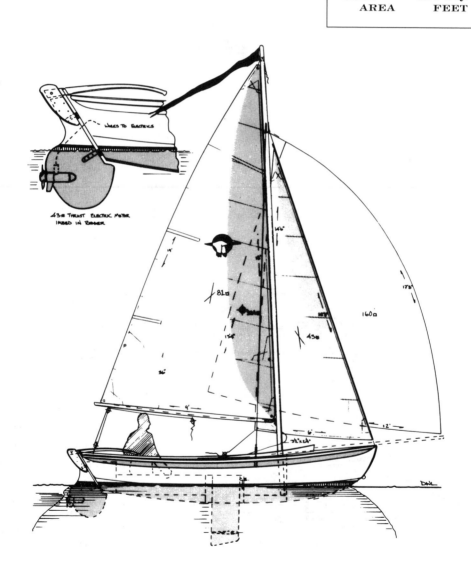

WINTER WREN

WINTER WREN	
L.O.A.	22'7"
L.O.D.	18'8"
L.W.L.	15'1"
BEAM	6'10"
DRAFT	2'6"
SAIL AREA	194 SQ. FEET

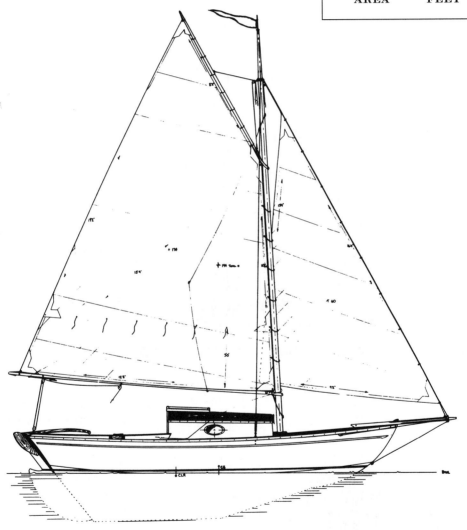

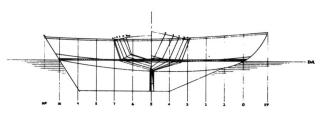

ARCTIC TERN

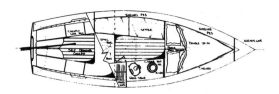

ARCTIC TERN	
L.O.D.	22'8"
L.W.L.	18'5"
BEAM	7'6"
DRAFT	3'1"
SAIL AREA	262 SQ. FEET

178

NODDY

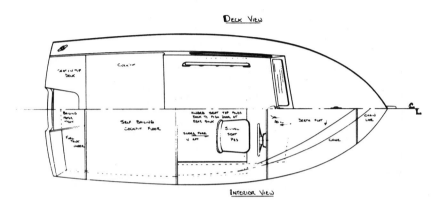

Deck View

Interior View

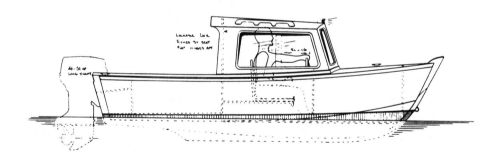

NODDY	
L.O.A.	15'11"
BEAM	7'10"
DRAFT	13"

DIPPER

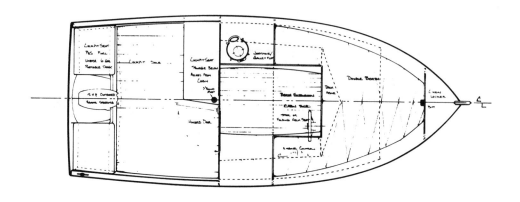

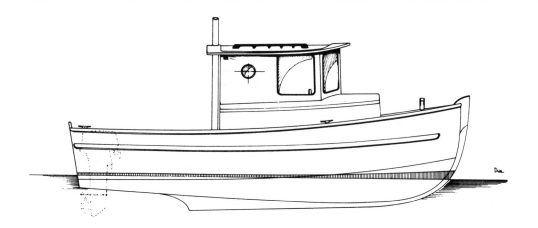

DIPPER	
L.O.A.	16'4"
BEAM	7'
DRAFT	1'8"
DISPLACEMENT	
	1300 LBS.

MILLIE HILL

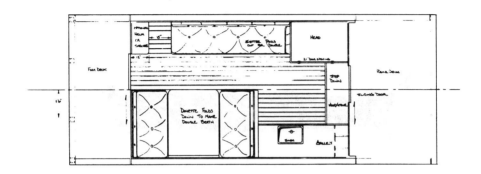

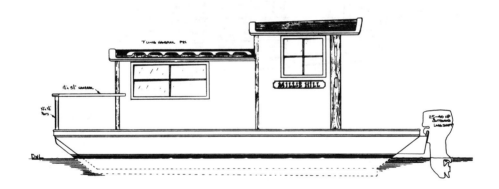

MILLIE HILL	
L.O.A.	20'0"
D.W.L.	17'5"
BEAM	8'2"
DRAFT	12"

SURF SCOTER

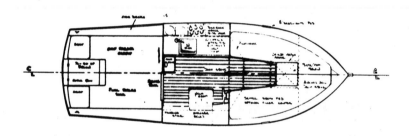

SURF SCOTER	
LENGTH	22'0"
D.W.L.	20'3"
BEAM	7'8"
DRAFT	1'11"

BLACK CROWN 29'

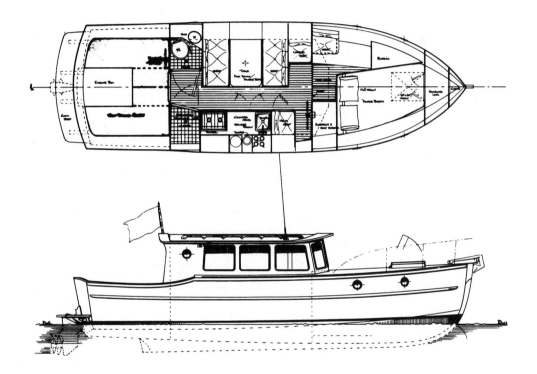

BLACK CROWN 29'	
LENGTH	29'2"
BEAM	10'
DRAFT	2'3"
DISPLACEMENT	8400 LBS.

CZARINNA 30'

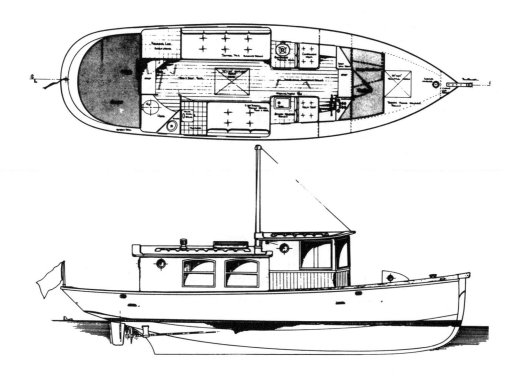

CZARINNA 30	
L.O.A.	29'10"
L.W.L.	25'3"
BEAM	8'6"
DRAFT	2'4"
DISPLACEMENT	
	8900 LBS.

BLUE PETER

BLUE PETER	
L.O.D.	30'2"
L.W.L.	24'8"
BEAM	9'3"
DRAFT	4'7"

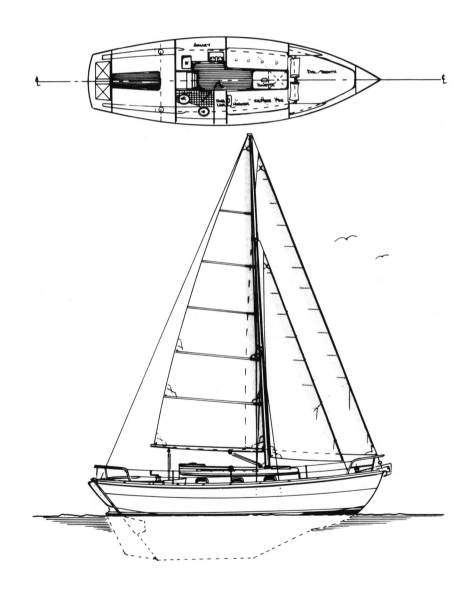

OYSTA 42'

OYSTA 42'	
LENGTH	42'1"
BEAM	12'1"
DRAFT	5'0"
L.W.L.	37'0"
DISPLACEMENT	
24,000 LBS.	

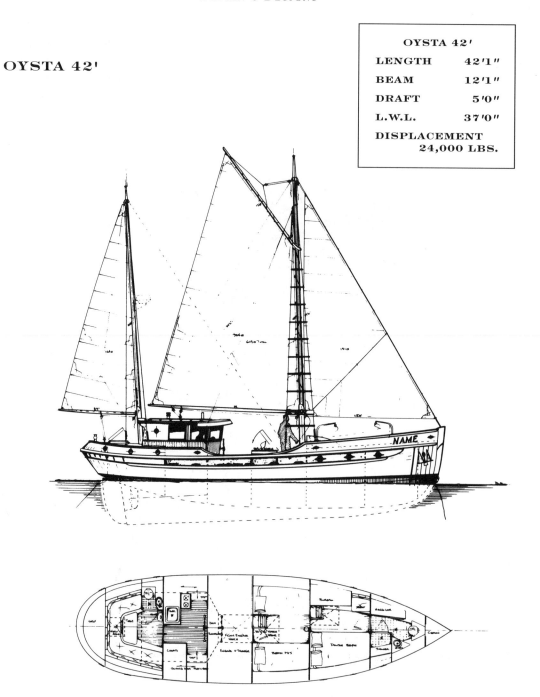

APPENDIX B

LIST OF SUPPLIERS

The following is not a complete list, but I believe all the suppliers listed to be reliable and dependable. Specialty marine, lumber, and tool companies often change hands or go out of business, and new ones are formed just as often. I include this list in the hope it will be helpful. Please don't hold me responsible for the pace of change in the 1990s. Finally, an important source for *me* in compiling this list was Bob Steward's *Boatbuilding Manual,* Fourth Edition (IM, 1994). Thanks to Bob and his excellent book.

Boatbuilding Plans

Many of the designers listed below offer brochures, catalogs, or both.

B.C.A./Demco Kit. 505 Via Riccarelli, 21-20148, Milano, Italy.

Ted Brewer Yacht Designs, Box 187, Lyman, WA 98263.

Complete Guide to Boat Kits & Plans, P.O. Box 540638, Merritt Island, FL 32954.

Devlin Designing Boatbuilders, 2424 Gravelly Beach Loop N.W., Olympia, WA 98502.

Glen-L Marine Designs, 9152 Rosecrans, Bellflower, CA 90706.

Hankinson Associates, P.O. Box 272, Hayden Lake, ID 83835.

IBIS Boatworks (Alan Chin), P.O. Box 65, Glen Huntly, VIC 3163, Australia

Norwalk Island Sharpies, 213 Rowayton Avenue, Rowayton, CT 06853.

H. H. ("Dynamite") Payson & Company, Pleasant Beach Road, South Thomaston, ME 04858.

Pygmy Kayaks, Jackson Street, Port Townsend, WA 98368.

Databoat Internat'l Ltd., Box 1073, 8609 Fissile Lane, Whistler, B.C., Canada V0N 1B0.

Island Boat Plans, 40 Belle Vue Rd., Cowes, Isle of Wight, P031 7HJ, England.

Tools and Hardware

Adjustable Clamp Company, 417 N. Ashland, Chicago, IL 60622. *Complete line of clamps under the "Jorgensen" and "Pony" brand names.*

Cascade Tools, Inc., P.O. Box 3110, Bellingham, WA 98227. *Router bits and drill bits.*

Albert Constantine & Sons, Inc., 2050 Eastchester Rd., Bronx, NY 10461, and Constantine's Wood Center, 1040 Oakland Park Boulevard, Ft. Lauderdale, FL 33334. *Distributors of tools, including taper-point drills for wood-screw holes and Japanese hand saws, chisels, planes, and waterstones; also carries finishing materials, interior joinerwork hardware, and abrasives.*

Fein Power Tools, Inc., 3019 W. Carson Street, Pittsburgh, PA 15204.

W.L. Fuller, Inc., 7 Cypress Street, Warwick, RI 02888. *Countersinks, counterbores, plug cutters, tapered drills.*

Garrett Wade Company, Inc., 161 Avenue of the Americas, New York, NY 10013. *Hardware and tools, including a large variety of Japanese hand tools.*

Gougeon Brothers, Inc., 706 Martin Street, Bay City, MI 48706. *An epoxy-supply firm that also sells the Scarffer, an attachment for a portable circular saw.*

Highland Hardware, 1045 N. Highland Avenue N.E., Atlanta, GA 30306. *Wide selection of woodworking tools (power and hand).*

John Henry Inc., P.O. Box 473, Spanish Fort, AL 36527. *The John Henry Planer-Scarffer Attachment.*

Wetzler Clamp Company, Rte. 611, Box 175, Mt. Bethel, PA 18343. *Complete line of clamps.*

Wilcox-Crittenden, Middletown, CT 06457. *Complete line of marine hardware, including navigation lights.*

Wood Carver's Supply, P.O. Box 8928, Norfolk, VA 23508. *Cutting tools.*

Woodcraft, 210 Wood County Industrial Park, Parkersburg, WV 26102-1686. *Japanese chisels, hand saws, waterstones, and slipstones.*

Boat Equipment Chandlers

Doc Freeman's, P.O. Box 300314, Seattle, WA 98103.

Fisheries Supply, 1900 N. Northlake Way, Seattle, WA 98103.

West Marine, 500 Westridge Drive, Watsonville, CA 95076.

Sails

Center Harbor Sails, Brooklin, ME 04616.

Lidgard Sails, 3507 Evanston Avenue N., Seattle, WA 98103.

Port Townsend Sails, 315 Jackson Street, Port Townsend, WA 98368.

Bronze Marine Hardware

ABI Industries, 415 Tamal Plaza, Corte Madera, CA 94925.

Bristol Bronze, P.O. Box 101, Bristol, RI 02878. *Specializes in reproductions of Herreshoff Manufacturing Company hardware.*

Bronze Star, Inc., 1235 Scott Street, San Diego, CA 92106.

Buck-Algonquin, 1565 Palmyra Bridge Road, Pennsauken, NJ 08110.

Marine Associates, 1651 Hanley Rd., Hudson, WI 54018. *Single-arm and V-propeller shaft struts, rudder ports, tiller arms, shaft logs, and stuffing boxes.*

New Found Metals, Inc., 240 West Airport Road, Port Townsend, WA 98368.

Port Townsend Foundry, 11 Crutcher Road, Port Townsend, WA 98368.

Simpson Lawrence USA, Inc., Box 11210, Bradenton, FL 34282-210. *Windlasses, CQR "plow" anchors, and other products made in Scotland.*

Spartan Marine, Hardware Division, Robinhood Marine Center, Robinhood, ME 04530. *Bronze and stainless steel hardware.*

Lumber, Plywood

Black Mountain Wood Company, P.O. Box 130, South Windham, ME 04082. *Hardwoods and pine; manufacturer of wood components.*

Boulter Plywood Corporation, 24 Broadway, Somerville, MA 02145. *Douglas fir, quarter-sawn or sliced teak and okoume marine plywood to British standards. Also solid lumber: teak, ash, Honduras mahogany, white oak, khaya, and premium vertical-grain Sitka spruce spar stock.*

M. L. Condon Company, Inc., 258 Ferris Avenue, White Plains, NY 10603. *Mast- and spar-grade Sitka spruce, Philippine and Honduras mahogany, white cedar, oak, teak, cypress, Alaska yellow cedar, Douglas fir, and lignum vitae; fir, teak, ash, mahogany, and imported Bruynzeel mahogany plywood.*

Albert Constantine & Sons, Inc., 2050 Eastchester Rd., Bronx, NY 10461. *Sells a meter for determining the moisture content of wood.*

Dean Company, P.O. Box 426, Gresham, OR 97030. *⅛"-thick veneer for cold-molded plankings.*

Edensaw Woods Ltd., 211 Seton Road, Port Townsend, WA 98368. *Teak, ironbark, mahoganies, Douglas fir, Alaska yellow cedar, and Western red cedar. Also Kelbrand marine plywood, to British standard 1088. Okoume or sapele faces with okoume core throughout; each panel subject to ultrasonic testing for ply lamination.*

Flounder Bay Boat Lumber, Third and O Streets, Anacortes, WA 98221; (206) 293-2369. *Marine plywood; dimensional boatbuilding lumber.*

Harbor Sales Company, 1400 Russell Street, Baltimore, MD 21230. *Teak, okoume, sapele, fir, lauan, waterproof plywood.*

Horsepower Logging Company (Tom Hamilton), RFD 1, Box 192, Cornville, ME 04976.

Hudson Marine Panels, Box 58, Ashley, PA 18706; Box 1184, Elkhart, IN 46515.

Lucky G. Farms, Box 5920, Hartland, ME 04943. *Hackmatack knees.*

Northwoods Canoe Shop, RFD 3, Box 118-2A, Dover-Foxcroft, ME 04426. *Canoe-building material including white cedar; also a VHS video made in their shop that covers wood bending, selection and preparation of wood, and construction of a steam box.*

Olyve Hardwoods, Wilmington, NC; (919) 686-4611. *Teak, marine plywood, mahogany, Atlantic white cedar; no minimum.*

Fred Tebb and Sons, Inc., 1906 Marc Street, Tacoma, WA 98421. *Sitka spruce specialists: wet or dry, rough or planed, various grades.*

West Wind Hardwoods, Inc., Box 2205, 10230 Bowerbank Road, Sidney, B.C. Canada V8L 358; (604) 656-0848. *Bruynzeel and domestic marine plywoods, Sitka spruce, fir, red and yellow cedar; distributor for Harbor Sales Company.*

Wooden Boat Shop, Seattle, WA; (206) 634-3600. *Marine plywood*

Fiberglass

Defender Industries, Inc., 255 Main Street, P.O. Box 820, New Rochelle, NY 10802-6544.

Erskine Johns, 4677 Worth Street, Los Angeles, CA 90063.

Metal and Plastic Fasteners

Chesapeake Marine Fasteners, P.O. Box 6521, Annapolis, MD 21401.

Copper Nail, P.O. Box 936, Sacramento, CA 95804. *Copper clench nails.*

Hamilton Marine, Route 1, Searsport, ME 04974.

Independent Nail Inc., Bridgewater, MA 02324. *Makers of Anchorfast nails.*

Jamestown Distributors, P.O. Box 348, Jamestown, RI 02835 and Rt. 1, Box 375, Seabrook, SC 29940. *All types of marine fasteners.*

Pacific Fasteners U.S., Inc., 2407 South 200th Street, P.O. Box 58304, Seattle, WA 98188. *Flathead silicon bronze wood screws with square socket heads in sizes ranging from #6 x ¾" to #14 x 3" long.*

Epoxy

Gougeon Brothers, Inc., P.O. Box 908, Bay City, MI 48707.

Industrial Formulators of Canada, Ltd., 3824 William Street, Burnaby, B.C., Canada. *G2 and Cold Cure epoxies.*

SP Systems, Blake's Marine Paints Ltd., Harbour Rd., Gosport, Hampshire, P012 1BQ.

Hankinson Associates, P.O. Box 272, Hayden Lake, ID 83835.

Matrix Adhesive Systems, 1501 Sherman Avenue, Pennsauken, NJ 08110. *High-tech epoxies for boatbuilding.*

System Three Resins, P.O. Box 70436, Seattle, WA 98107.

Deck and Companionway Hatches

Bomar, Inc., Box W, Charlestown, NH 03603.

Go Industries, 20331 Lake Forest Drive, Unit C14, El Toro, CA 92630.

Taco Supply, 1495 N.E. 129th Street, North Miami, FL 33161 and 18870 72nd Avenue South, Kent, WA 98032.

Windows

American Marine, 1790 SW 13th Court, Pompano Beach, FL 33069.

B & J Aluminum Windows, Route 5, Box 4812, St. Martinville, LA 70582. *Heavy-duty metal windows.*

Noncorrosive Locks

Phoenix Lock Company, 321 Third Avenue, Newark, NJ 07107-2392.

Abrasives

Albert Constantine & Sons, Inc., 2050 Eastchester Rd., Bronx, NY 10461.

The Sanding Catalog, P.O. Box 3737, Hickory, NC 28603-3737.

One-Off or Production Castings of Lead

Mars Metal, 4130 Morris Drive, Burlington, ON, Canada L7L 5L6.

Willard, 101 New Bern Street, Charlotte, NC 28203.

Aluminum Alloy Spars

Dwyer Aluminum Mast Company, 21 Commerce Drive, North Branford, CT 06471.

Hall Rigging, 17 Peckham Drive, Bristol, RI 02829.

Kenyon Marine, New Whitfield Street, Guilford, CT 06437.

Taco Supply, 1495 N.E. 129th Street, North Miami, FL 33161, and 18870 72nd Avenue South, Kent, WA 98032.

Spar Tech Co., 5230 N.E. 92nd Street, Redmond, WA 98052-3518

Wooden Yacht Blocks

Bainbridge Blocks, 1481 Shoemakersville Rd., Shoemakersville, PA 19555.

Finished ash shell blocks; also kits for do-it-yourself finishing and assembly.
Pert Lowell Company, Inc., Lane's End, Newbury, MA 01951.

Hydraulic Steering Components

Hynautic, Inc., 1579 Barber Road, Sarasota, FL 34240.
Teleflex, Inc., 640 North Lewis Road, Limerick, PA 19468.
Wagner Marine (USA) Inc., 14326 102nd Street N.E., Bothell, WA 98011.

Engine Controls

Edson International, 460 Industrial Park Road, New Bedford, MA 02745-1292. *Control heads.*
Kobelt Manufacturing Company, Ltd., 11720 Horseshoe Way, Richmond, BC, Canada V7A 4V5. *Control heads.*
Morse Controls, 21 Clinton Street, Hudson, OH 44236. *Control heads; push-pull cables.*
Teleflex, Inc., 640 North Lewis Road, Limerick, PA 19468. *Push-pull cables.*

Circuit Breaker Panels

Heritage Panel Graphics, 5710 200th Street SW, #307, Lynnwood, WA 98036-6257.
Marinetics Corporation, P.O. Box 2676, Newport Beach, CA 92663.

Oars, Paddles, Oarlocks

Barkley Sound Marine, 3073 Vanhorne Road, Qualicum Beach, BC, Canada V9K 1X3.
Shaw & Tenney, 20 Water Street, P.O. Box 213, Orono, ME 04473.

The WoodenBoat Store, P.O. Box 78, Brooklin, ME 04616. *Plans for making oars, as well as a leather-and-button kit with instructions and enough leather and fasteners for one pair of oars.*

Steering

Edson International, 460 Industrial Park Road, New Bedford, MA 02745-1292.

Water Trap Vent

Nicro Marine, 2065 West Avenue 140th, San Leandro, CA 94577.

Tanks

Tempo Products Company, P.O. Box 39126, Cleveland, OH 44139. *Stock metal and nonmetallic tanks.*
Vetus Den Ouden, Inc., P.O. Box 8712, Baltimore, MD 21240-0712. *Stock nonmetallic tanks.*

Computer Lofting Services

Aerohydro, Inc., P.O. Box 684, Main Street, Southwest Harbor, ME 04679.
Vacanti Yacht Design Software, 17226 163rd Place SE, Renton, WA 98058.
Specialty Marine Contractors, P.O. Box 1081, Scappoose, OR 97056.

Respirators

3M Occupational Health & Safety Products Division, 1-800-328-1300. *Extensive line of respirators.*

Safety Information

U.S. Coast Guard, Office of Boating Safety, Washington, DC 20590.

INDEX

Note: **Boldface** type indicates illustration.